THE INVISIBLE BACKPACK

The Adventures of Dakota Stone

by
JB Woak

PublishAmerica
Baltimore

ISBN: 978-1-4489-5569-5
PUBLISHED BY PUBLISHAMERICA, LLLP
www.publishamerica.com
Baltimore

Printed in the United States of America

To My Brother,
Arthur
Who always put my needs and safety before his own.
You will always be my hero.

ACKNOWLEDGMENTS

No project comes together by the efforts of just one person. In my case, there were many who were instrumental in bringing this book to completion. First, I owe the largest thank you to my editor, Ricky Bourque, who always knew when to praise, when to challenge, and when to support. She became my coach, mentor, and friend. Her knowledge and experience in the publishing field were invaluable.

Many thoughts of appreciation go to my husband, Michael, whose support and encouragement helped me to capture and articulate my ideas. His understanding as I spent hours alone with my computer also helped to make this book a reality.

Thanks to Lupe Tovar and Hugo Torres for keeping me real and connected to the needs of the ones for whom I wrote this book—the children and grown children who have not had the advantage of a supportive family and therefore missed "the quest."

I am blessed with many great friends who contributed in countless ways to this effort: Thanks to La Jaun Dunn, Suzan Ragan, Sue Carder, Helene Nelson, Virginia Diggs, Christa Drake, Cathleen Fitzgerald, Renee Curren, and Amie Goldman for their love, support, and encouragement. Michael and Sabrina Knowles, thanks for your friendship and technical assistance. A heartfelt appreciation goes out to Captain David Kauffman for opening the doors for this book to move forward.

Contents

PREFACE

THE AUTHOR'S INVISIBLE BACKPACK

Research has proven that grandparents can have an important positive impact on the lives of others within and out of the family circle.

Hi! I'm J.B. Woak, but you can call me Grandma. I like being called Grandma because it has a family ring to it, and I have had a lifetime full of experiences. Because of those experiences I can encourage younger generations in ways to endure trouble times. I may even have the opportunity to pass on some good principles and values to build strong character.

A grandmother represents the past and present, and I have been around for a while. Like me, no matter how young you are, you have a past. So often, we carry our past burdens with us for the rest of our lives. This reminds me of an invisible backpack, I carry one with me all the time. Let me explain it this way.

Have you ever carried a heavy backpack? How did it make you feel? Did it slow you down or hold you back? Did your backpack ever get on your nerves? Maybe you couldn't wait to get rid of it. Did it prevent you from standing tall? Did you envy others who had a lighter backpack?

My invisible backpack stores all my experiences and scars from my past. The rocks in my backpack represent the negative behaviors and attitudes I developed as a child in order to survive. I was unaware that the defensive behaviors and attitudes I used to survive in childhood would influence my daily life in the future. At some point in my adult life I had to take ownership and responsibility for my life, even when it had been mismanaged by others. Breaking free involves getting rid of any negative baggage that put limits on my potential.

This is when my real life expedition began. This is not any easy task. Changing what's rooted in my backpack is a lifelong quest.

I know the feeling and the reality of coming from a non-supportive family. I felt the shame of abuse and the scars from neglect. I have experienced the uncertainty of being in foster care and the insecurity that comes with each move. I know the feeling of not wanting to develop relationships, because I didn't know when I would have to move again. I knew I was different from my peers. They had parents to call Mom and Dad, and I had social workers and foster parents that I called by their first names.

The transition into adulthood was difficult for me. I had no idea of what "normal" was. I became solely responsible for my live overnight without a supportive family, and without the necessary life skills to live on my own. Without the right ingredients, I would face tremendous challenges in adulthood.

As a young adult I didn't understand all the emotional baggage from my past had followed me into adulthood. But I did realize that the biggest part of overcoming my past would be to acquire knowledge. I did this in many ways. I learned from others who have walked in my shoes, and from books that both inspired me and gave me new life skills. Look for the list at the back of this book for some of them. There you will find many great authors and the titles of their books that were valuable to me during my quest for knowledge.

Along with knowledge I would need faith to believe in my ability to handle the difficult times. Faith is about knowing that even when you can't see the sun, it will still come up tomorrow.

Coming from a non-supportive family isn't for wimps. I like the story Bob Hope told about his mother. He said, "My mother washed my clothes by beating them against a rock, with me in them." In my childhood there were many situations that beat me up.

Who were the first contributors to my rock collection? That would be my parents, and later they were any persons of authority whose

10

responsibility it was to nurture and care for me. These are the people who completely let me down, and my emotional baggage was a high price to pay for their neglect and abuse.

My story will take you through three stages of my early life. The first stage will describe the first ten years, the second stage will cover the next five years, and the last stage will tell you about my years from sixteen through eighteen.

First ten years

My mother was an alcoholic and illiterate. She was 35 when I was born. My father was on his third marriage and had spent time in prison before marrying my mother. He was 45 when I was born. My parents never got divorced even though they were separated most of my life. I had a brother, Arthur, who was a year older, and we were very close.

I was born in Ohio, but my childhood memories start at the age of five while living in the small town of Greenwood, South Carolina. Little did I know that the size of my backpack was about to change.

My father left us to return to Ohio and reunite with his second wife and their two teenage sons. Soon after, my third half-brother was born. I didn't know them until I left foster care.

When I was six years old, my mother decided to hitchhike to Ohio, with my brother and me, to find our father. It must have been extremely difficult for her to be homeless, uneducated, and have two young children. Soon after reaching Ohio, she placed Arthur and me in foster care. I'm sure she thought that she was making the best choice at the time.

This was a scary time for me. Fortunately, I had my brother. Our first foster home was on a farm. Arthur and I lived there until I was nine years old. The foster family had two of their own children and one other foster child.

On the day of our arrival, some of the family members were working in the fields. Arthur was sent to work there, and I was to help with the household chores. I panicked. I didn't want my brother to leave me, so I ran after him, only to be returned to the house. I was warned that I could get lost or be bitten by snakes. When I took off again, I was locked in a bedroom. I climbed out of the window and headed in the direction I had last seen my brother. I was angry—I felt they were taking Arthur away from me. When I saw him return from the fields, I finally understood that my brother wasn't leaving.

It didn't take long to adjust to my new environment. I was learning where I fit in. Along with daily farm work, the foster parents were janitors at the local school, and all the children helped with those chores. There were good times, too. We played baseball, rode horseback, and went swimming in a river that flowed through the farm. We also attended many church activities.

When school started, I was in first grade. Unfortunately, school would become a disruptive force in my life. I was dyslexic, although no one recognized it. I remember studying for a spelling test. The eldest daughter was trying to help me with the words. She became frustrated with my impaired ability to learn quickly, and she accused me of playing dumb and not listening. Once I had a part in a school play. I worked hard to learn my lines, but when it came time to deliver them, I couldn't remember the words. I was told I was an embarrassment to the family. I didn't understand why I was being criticized, so I decided never to try that again. I began to believe I wasn't intelligent and it was somehow my fault. Verbal abuse doesn't leave bruises, but it can leave scars that last for many years.

Since I couldn't adjust to a condition I didn't understand, I acted out by lying and using other negative behaviors. I was labeled a problem child. During this time, more rocks were added to my backpack collection—low self-esteem, fear of appearing stupid, and fear of failing.

When I was seven years old, I was molested by the foster father. Another authority figure had failed me. How could I feel safe in this home? I was afraid and embarrassed, and I felt powerless. I thought I was being punished for some reason. I didn't tell anyone. I felt that it must have been my fault. The rocks of shame and guilt were added to my backpack.

When I was nine, the foster system returned Arthur and me to our biological dysfunctional family. Whenever I had to live with my parents, the results were always negative. Living with them just added to the obstacles I would have to overcome later in life.

My father forced me to help him steal. Even as a child, I had an inner battle with this, and I was confused. In Sunday school, I had been taught that stealing was wrong. I loved my father, but I hated what I was forced to do. I was afraid that if I offended him, he wouldn't love me or he might leave us again.

I will never forget the day my father took me shoplifting for a new pair of shoes. My role was to hold open a shopping bag while he slipped the shoes inside the bag. When we were caught, I was so terrified. My father was jailed, and the police took me to my mother.

My father gave me the rock of misplaced loyalty. I had to choose between doing what I knew was right or obeying my father.

For the next few months, Arthur and I were passed around to different family members. For some reason, my aunts and uncles always gave us back to our mother. More than once, we found her in a bar. I remember thinking it must be our fault because nobody wanted us. My mother was living with her boyfriend at the time. He also was alcoholic, and I'm sure he wasn't happy about two children becoming a part of his life.

One day my mother heard a knock on the door. She quickly hid Arthur and me in the closet under some blankets. I never knew who was at the door, but she left and she never returned. The man who owned the home eventually locked us out and the streets became our home. After several months of sleeping under porches and in empty houses, the police picked us up. They didn't have a home for us, so they placed us in a detention facility. Arthur and I were immediately separated and I was placed in an 8'x10' cell. I didn't like this at all, and it didn't take long for me to express my displeasure. Being separated from my brother was the worst thing that could have happened to me at that time. It was even worse than living on the streets. He was my protector and the only one I could trust.

I looked forward to mealtimes, when I could escape my cell for a little while. In the dining area, I got to see Arthur. We were not allowed to sit together, (girls and boys were separated there), but I knew Arthur was close by.

After breakfast and a shower, I was permitted to get a book, magazine, or puzzle to take back to the cell. There was no playtime or

13

even a TV to watch. Some of the children had visitors, but no one came to visit me.

Can you imagine being nine years old and locked in an 8'x10' cell with only a bed, desk, chair, and toilet?

I was devastated when my brother was able to leave the detention facility before I did. He was my only real connection to the world. Without Arthur, I had no one who even cared that I was there. It was as if I didn't exist. I cried and asked God to find me a home. The bars on the window and the lock on the door made me feel empty and alone. The rock of anger was always just below the surface, waiting to explode. I added the rocks of rejection, resentment, and bitterness to my collection. At the age of ten, all the hurt, pain, neglect, and abuse were hidden in my invisible backpack. With the added emotional baggage, it appeared that I needed a bigger backpack.

Let's review my collection of rocks:

Low self-esteem and lack of self-worth	Anger
Fear of failure	Guilt
Fear of uncertainly	Shame
Fear of being alone	Resentment
Fear of rejection	Bitterness

I didn't know how to channel or even begin to understand the trauma that created this list.

I learned to develop defensive behaviors to protect myself from things I didn't comprehend. These survival behaviors were an automatic response—I didn't even think about it. I became aggressive at any injustice done to me. When a girl in school blamed me for something I didn't do, I caught her alone in the restroom and beat her up. I even took on the boys. This aggressive behavior got me into a lot of trouble, but I developed a false sense of security in knowing I was taking care of myself regardless of the consequence.

Here are a few of the survival behaviors I developed:

Being aggressive over any injustice

Using denial as a mask to hide insecurities and faults

Being defensive and overly sensitive when criticized or rejected

Using victim behaviors—blaming others, self-pity, and dependent on others for happiness

Being a people pleaser, trying to live up to others' expectations

Being a troublemaker, rebelling against authority figures

Being manipulative: sometimes just telling people what they wanted to hear

These behaviors added more weight to my backpack and had a negative influence on my life.

Ages 11 to 15

After leaving the dentition home, I was placed in three different foster homes and then placed back in the detention facility. The three foster homes were difficult for me. I missed my brother, and I didn't seem able to adjust to my new surroundings. My backpack may have been invisible, but the rocks in it were determining my actions. My survival behaviors were creating many problems for me. I just didn't know it.

At the age of twelve, I was placed in my fourth foster home. I had lived there before; it was where I was molested. Whenever I was left alone with the foster father, he would taunt and threaten me. He knew I was afraid of him. One night when I was left alone with him, I hid outside in the dark until the rest of the family returned. I was frightened of the dark and its eerie sounds, but I was more frightened of him. I kept my distance from him, and no one knew that he had molested me. There was no one I could talk to. At some point, I couldn't handle the fear any more, and I decided to run away. I walked until I was tired and afraid of the dark. I finally went to a house and asked for help. They called the police, who took me back to the detention facility. I ended up in the same cell I had when I was nine. I felt powerless and misunderstood. What had I done wrong? Why was this happening to me? The injustice seemed so overwhelming. I felt like a caged animal, filled with hate, resentment, and anger. On top of that, I felts no one would listen to my complaints or believe me.

In the detention facility, I was told that if I didn't straighten up I would be placed in a girls' correctional facility. I had a lot of time to think about my next placement, and I decided that my actions and reactions needed to change. I had to learn to please other people.

I lived in my fifth foster home for three years, until I was fifteen years old. I was happy there because there was no foster father in the home and I could relax. I seemed to be well liked in the new role of people pleaser, but people pleasing turned out to be a huge rock that often left me feeling confused. I was accepted and appreciated, but only when I complied with what was expected of me.

Ages 16 through 18

The next few years were some of the most damaging times in my life. This time, the abuse again came from my birth family. When I was sixteen, the system sent me back to my father. I cried because I didn't want to leave my foster home. How could the foster care system do this to me? My father didn't have the money to support us, but I was happy to be reunited with my brother. Arthur helped my father steal food from unlocked cars, but he would not allow my father to force me to steal. I was so grateful for that.

After a few months, my father sent me to live with family members, while Arthur decided to live with our mother. I felt that he was choosing to leave me. Again I felt rejected.

But I was happy in my new home. I got along with the five children except the eldest daughter. She was jealous and told her mother that if I didn't go, she would leave. I lived there only a short time, and it broke my heart to leave. I was sent to live with my father's second wife, the woman he had left us for while we lived in South Carolina. Here I met my three half-brothers. I wasn't there long either because I was raped by a family member. After the rape, I ran and hid under some bushes in the corner of the yard. I stayed there all night and cried. I was afraid to tell the police. I thought that surely I would be locked up, like before. When I felt it was safe, I went back to the house and called my father. He picked me up, and I went to live with a couple he knew. I didn't tell my father about the rape. I don't know if any more rocks were added to my backpack, but some of the old rocks became heavier.

I want to take a moment here to talk about rape. I personally refuse to take ownership of the rape. It was not my fault and I did not ask for it. I took my power back when I decided to remove any negative emotions I felt about myself or any behaviors that were the results of that incident. It can be hard to think or talk about a frightening experience, especially something as personal as rape. If there is something painful in your past, I urge you to assign the responsibility to its rightful owner and focus on the power to change. Don't be afraid to ask for help.

Later, my father's friends were arrested, and I was sent to live in a group home. This was the first time I lived in a dorm setting. I didn't do well there, and the other girls didn't like me. Being a people pleaser didn't work for me that time. I was confused about what role I should play. I didn't fit in, so I shut down and stayed to myself. I didn't have any friends, and I felt so alone.

At 17 ½, I was sent back to my father. We lived above a bar, and there always were drunks in the hallway. One evening I drove my father to work, and on the way home the car broke down. I managed to pull into a gas station and the attendant offered to take me home.

When we reached the apartment, he stopped but wouldn't let me out of the car. I fought back, but he was too strong. A friend came by and saw what was happening. My friend hit the car with his fist, and I was able to escape. My friend and I walked to the police station and told them what happened. Because I was under 18, they said my father would have to press charges. I explained to my father what had happened and that the guy tried to force himself on me. My father did talk to the police, but at some point the guy told my father I came on to him. He gave my father a large sum of money to drop the charges. My father blamed me for what had happened and he accepted the money. I hated my father for that.

My father asked his friend to talk me into becoming a prostitute. I was deeply hurt, and I refused to compromise my beliefs. That was the final straw. My relationship with my father was over, and I left the minute I turned eighteen.

I found my brother Arthur, who was living with our mother. He told me that the area they lived in was not safe, and he recommended that I live with a family member. I told him that this family member had raped me. Arthur told me that we had no other options and he would go with me to protect me. I always felt safe with him; but again, this family member made sexual advances toward me. Arthur defended me, and we left.

With no safe place to go, we stayed in an abandoned house. I had only a few weeks of high school left, so I continued to go to classes. I got my diploma while we were living in the abandoned house. Again, my brother stole food and clothing for me. I think I might have been one of the best-dressed girls in high school.

A neighbor saw us in the abandoned house and took me in until I could find an apartment to live in with my mother. Arthur joined the military and sent money to our mother to help pay for the rent.

After spending a day looking for work, I returned to an empty apartment. My mother and all the furniture were gone. Fortunately, I started my first job. With the help of the Salvation Army I was able pay the rent.

My brother was given a dishonorable discharge from the military. He had a hard time holding a job, and later in life he spent time in prison. Arthur became missing one day and was never found. I believe that he is dead. We were always close, and he would never have left without saying goodbye. I love my brother and miss him deeply. He was the only person in my life who protected me. He took care of me at his own expense.

At age 18, my backpack was still invisible to me, but hidden rocks of the past seemed to weigh me down. I could feel the heaviness in my heart—a heaviness I couldn't explain. I had feelings of hopelessness and despair. I had a lost sense of identity and looked for love and happiness in all the wrong places. I wanted love, respect, and approval, but often I came up empty with feelings of being used, misunderstood, and unappreciated. There was always something or someone that seemed to get in the way of my happiness.

What would be the logical way for me to view the world, considering the negative experiences during my childhood? Would I:

Trust others?

Want close relationships? Or would I build walls to protect myself?

Have high self-esteem or self-confidence?

Become a people pleaser just to get some form of acceptance?

Become a perfectionist, driving myself even harder?

Face adversity, or run from it?

Become protective and defensive to hide my insecurities?

Blame God?

It would take many years before I could understand and overcome the brokenness of my past. Finally I realized that if it's to be, it's up to me to take back what was stolen from me. Even though I had no control over the circumstances that were given to me, ultimately I had to accept that I am responsible for my life.

In order to find meaning in my life, I started a quest for knowledge. My first step was to go through the process of self-discovery. The next step of my journey was to take ownership of my life through self-empowerment. Only then was I able to turn my rocks into gems.

I hope my backpack story has encouraged you to examine your own backpack.

WHAT IS A QUEST?

It's a search for something and it's usually a long and difficult journey. When I think of a quest, I often think of an Indiana Jones movie. Your quest is not about finding ancient artifacts or gold. Your quest is to find knowledge and wisdom to create the life you desire. Each person's circumstances are unique but the steps to find happiness are the same for everyone.

Looking for happiness outside one's self is a fool's quest.

The pursuit of a happy and productive life is one of the greatest quests of a lifetime. Many people try to find it without understanding how to achieve it. The truth is, the elements that make the poor unhappy are the same elements that make the rich unhappy. Both believe that the outer packaging is more important than the inner person. If you look for the answers outside yourself, you may be taking a fool's quest.

Happiness that comes from within is not based on status, a bank book, possessions, talent, fame, beauty, sex, drugs, alcohol or controlling behaviors. This type of living leads to disappointments and the benefits are short lived. Seeking happiness in the wrong places is neither fun nor productive.

Would a fish be happy out of the water? I don't think so, because a fish was created to live in water. Our Creator created us to live from the inside out. It's where we begin to take responsibility for or choices, attitudes, behavior, beliefs and actions. Armed with knowledge and wisdom, we are able to move forward and change the direction of our life.

Supportive Family

When life gives you lemons, make lemonade. This only works if you know how to make lemonade. Once you have the recipe, the choice to follow it is up to you.

One of the main ingredients to becoming a productive happy adult starts with having a supportive family. Supportive families teach children how to function in the world. In a supportive surrounding, children are taught how to communicate their wants and needs, how to cope with conflict, how to resist peer pressure, how to achieve their goals and how to seek spiritual direction. Without these skills, they are at a disadvantage in creating a healthy lifestyle.

While no family is perfect, they play an important role in shaping the person we become. When parents are unable to meet the emotional needs of their children, their children become emotionally wounded. Actually what happens to us in our childhood has a big affect on our life. Emotionally wounded children grow up and become emotional wounded adults.

Did you come from an unsupportive family or a broken home? Perhaps your family was dysfunctional. Are you looking for happiness in the wrong places, only to find yourself misunderstood, used, or unappreciated? Maybe, you feel life isn't fair, that it's out of control or you don't understand the events that brought you to this place in your life.

Do you have difficulty achieving your goals? Are your relationships not working, or are you drifting from relationship to relationship, hoping the next one will be different? Do you try to control everything or maybe you are attracted to needy people and think you can fix their problems. Do you harbor secrets about your past?

If you are striving to improve the quality of your life, it is my pleasure to invite you to join Dakota Stone for an exciting adventure. Pack your bags and let's get started.

THE ADVENTURES
OF DAKOTA STONE

You are about to embark on an adventurous quest with Dakota Stone

Dakota's adventure is a quest to find the hidden mysteries of life that so far have eluded him. His quest will challenge him both physically and mentally.

Dakota will travel back through time to learn how his past experiences—the rocks in his backpack—have weighed down his present experiences. He will discover new ways of approaching life, and he will change the harmful rocks into gems.

As you travel with Dakota on his quest, discover who you are, where you are, and who you want to become. Observe and collect information that is relevant not only to Dakota's life, but perhaps your own. It takes guts and determination to navigate through the past, but the rewards are worth the effort.

SELF-DISCOVERY
THE INNER SELF

CHAPTER ONE

THE QUEST BEGINS

Commencement day at the university!
Dakota Stone settled himself against the broad trunk of his favorite tree outside the campus auditorium. He had more than an hour to himself before joining the other graduates for the commencement exercises.

He loved this tree. During his years at the university, he'd gone to its cool, green shelter whenever he needed a quiet place to solve a problem or sort through his thoughts. He always felt calm and safe sitting under this tree. It was as if the tree were spreading its sturdy branches to welcome him with a soft, leafy embrace. He needed its peace and comfort now.

"I've been working toward this day for a long time," he reflected. "Now that it's finally here, why am I not as happy as I expected I'd be?"

Dakota closed his eyes and thought about the 21 years of his life. It hadn't been an easy 21 years.

When he was six years old, Dakota had been removed from an abusive and dysfunctional family and placed in foster care. Unfortunately, life in foster care was as unstable as it had been with his birth family.

Over the next twelve years, Dakota was placed in ten different homes. The experience left him with the feeling that he didn't really "belong" anywhere. Mistakenly, he blamed himself for the moves. Each time, he wondered what terrible thing he had done to be moved from one family to another. He found it difficult to establish new relationships, and he was lonely. He knew he was different from other kids who had supportive families, and he struggled to find his place in a world he didn't understand.

Learning to read and write was easy, but after the third move to a new placement, he fell behind in his studies. Hiring a tutor was out of the question—it would be an extra expense. Luckily, he was blessed with the ability to learn quickly, and soon he was able to make up the work and catch up to his classmates. But with the next move and another new school, again he fell behind, and again he had to work hard to catch up.

The high school years were especially hard for Dakota. The welfare system continued to provide the basics—shelter, food, and clothing— and for that he was grateful. But he resented the fact that for the most part, the system ignored him as a person. He felt powerless. Case workers and other adults didn't listen to his wants and needs, nor did they involve him in decision making. They refused him the opportunity to be a kid. He hadn't been allowed to join the band or get involved in sports—there wasn't extra money for the equipment. How unfair that he wasn't permitted to get a driver's license at 16. Without a driver's license, he wasn't able to work outside the foster home; and without a job, he didn't have spending money like the other kids.

When he was 16, his social worker introduced him to Jesse Patterson, a Christian mentor. Jesse's role in Dakota's life was to be a supportive adult who would help him make the transition to independent living when he aged out of the system. Jesse would have two years to build a relationship with Dakota and gain his trust.

With Jesse's guidance, Dakota was able to overcome many of his resentments and learn new coping skills. He knew that many foster youth drop out of school and run away from the system, and he knew that if it hadn't been for Jesse's friendship and encouragement, he might have run away, too.

Jesse was always there for him. When Dakota was ready to transition out of foster care, Jesse taught Dakota how to develop a budget, maintain a checkbook, and fill out a job application. But most of all, Jesse gave him a reason to look forward to the future. Jesse gave him hope and a goal.

Dakota remembered the day Jesse asked him to memorize three words—have, do, be. Those three words had changed Dakota's life forever. He recalled their exact conversation.

"Dakota," said Jesse, "Decide what it is that you want to have in life. It can be anything."

"I want to be able to provide for myself and have a family someday," he answered.

"Okay, Dakota, in order to have what you want to have, you must decide what it is you must do to have it."

"I would have to accept the fact that I have to stay in foster care and not run away. I would have to get good grades and finish high school so I can go to college."

"That sounds like a good start," Jesse replied. "Now, what type of person do you have to be in order to accomplish your goal?"

Dakota remembered smiling at Jesse and saying, "I will need the willpower and desire to study. I will have to give up watching TV before my homework is finished. Once I'm out of foster care and on my own, I will need to be disciplined enough to say 'no' to others and sometimes give up hanging out with my friends."

"There you have it! Effort, choices, and action are what will make it happen. It's as simple as have, do, and be. The choice is completely up to you."

Dakota felt he could accomplish his goal, but he knew how difficult it would be to stay focused. Nevertheless, he made a commitment to Jesse to give it his best.

Jesse assured him he would be there to help him through the difficult times. He asked Dakota to visualize how his life would be different when he graduated from college.

And he had followed through! Today was commencement day!

Dakota heard laughter and was jolted back to the moment. Families were beginning to arrive for the commencement activities. They looked so happy—taking pictures, hugging each other, congratulating the graduates. A sudden wave of loneliness swept over him and he felt the emptiness of not having a family to share his success. All at once, he realized that he couldn't go through with the commencement ceremony. He would ask that his diploma be mailed to him. As he watched the proud families and the happy graduates, he knew he had made the right decision. He stood up, brushed off his clothes, and slowly walked off the campus for the last time.

As he walked away, he was happy that Jesse had invited him to have dinner with his family to celebrate the graduation. Dakota didn't want a party. His friends would be celebrating with their families and friends—and along with everything else, his girlfriend had just broken up with him.

"Another relationship gone sour," he thought to himself. "Why can't I seem to maintain relationships?"

After dinner, Dakota played games with Jesse's children. He loved Jesse's two lively sons. Being with them had always brought out the child in him.

"Hey, boys, you're going to wear Dakota out! Give him a break!" Jesse laughed. "Dakota let's go out to the patio where we can talk."

They seated themselves comfortably on the cool patio. "Dakota," Jesse said, "do you know how proud I am of you? You have sacrificed so much to achieve this goal. You held down a job, and still made excellent grades. I know how hard it was to give up personal time with your friends. I know they teased you for staying home and studying. But you have reached your goal and you have two job offers for the fall. Are you thinking about taking the job in Australia, or will you stay here in the states?"

"I'm not sure right now," Dakota answered. "I have a few months to make that decision. But I need your help with another challenge. No matter how much I've accomplished, I still have emptiness inside, and I don't know how to get rid of it. I feel alone, and I'm afraid of the future. How can I ever create a happy family when I can't maintain a relationship? I always find a way to mess things up and they leave. That's the story of my life. Everyone always leaves. Well—except you, Jesse.

"I know I have a lot of emotional baggage, but I don't know how to overcome it. But I see how you and your family get along, and I know it's something I want. I don't know what 'normal' is, and I'm tired of walking around pretending how happy I am. Before coming here, I watched the families gather for commencement. It hurt deeply, and I wanted to be a part of something I can never have. That moment has passed me by forever. I will never be able to experience the joy of sharing my graduation with family or loved ones. What have I worked so hard for if there isn't someone to share it with? I don't want to grow old and be alone, but I don't want to get married and end up divorced. I don't want to put my children through that pain."

Jesse's voice softened. "I understand, Dakota. I have been in your shoes. I know that emptiness. Let me try to explain it as best I can.

"We all have an invisible backpack that holds our past experiences, both good and bad. Within our backpack is where our wounded child lives. The child had to learn to survive in an unhealthy environment. Because of this, the wounded child defends and protects itself in dysfunctional ways. I guess you can say we have an unhealthy relationship with ourselves and we don't know it."

Dakota agreed. "That makes sense. If we have an unhealthy relationship with ourselves, how can we deal with others in a healthy way?"

"You're asking the right question," said Jesse. "To rescue your wounded child, you must go on an expedition, a quest for the right direction. The expedition is a lot like an Indiana Jones movie. The objective is always to find something rare and of great value. The quest always begins with acquiring a map to locate the treasure. To make it more interesting, the map is often like a puzzle. There is always missing information which requires Indiana to make a decision or take a risk. He doesn't go it alone—he always finds people with the knowledge to help him. He has to be open to change, and if his choices are faulty, they may threaten his life. Mistakes usually require him to revisit his map and make new choices.

"Like Indy, you need a strong desire and commitment to face each challenge and resist the urge to turn back when the going gets tough. There will be mistakes along the way, but a determined explorer never gives up. Explorers don't waste energy on the past, but focus only on what lies ahead."

"That all sounds great, but where do I start this quest?" asked Dakota anxiously.

Jesse stepped inside the house, and when he returned he handed Dakota an envelope.

"What's this?" Dakota asked.

Jesse smiled. "This is your graduation gift. I bought this for you a month ago. I had a feeling you would need it."

Dakota opened the envelope and discovered an airline ticket to Spain!

"I don't understand," he said. "It's a one-way ticket."

"Don't worry about that," Jesse replied. "It's not easy to determine when you will finish your quest. The return ticket will be provided after you complete your quest."

"But why do I need to go to Spain?" asked a still confused Dakota.

"Spain is the starting point. There you will begin your quest to rescue your wounded child from the past. Your journey will take you through territory you have never explored before. Your mission is to find learning nuggets that will present themselves along the way. Each learning nugget will contain valuable knowledge and wisdom that will guide you through the mysteries of life. You will travel to many places. At each location, you must make a list of the learning nuggets you have gathered there. When you are ready to leave for your next destination, a gatekeeper will examine the list and determine whether you can continue. If the gatekeeper is satisfied that your list is complete and you have learned everything offered at that location, he will unlock the gate and direct you to your next destination." Jesse took a small chest from the patio table behind him and placed it in Dakota's hands. "Before he unlocks the gate, you will place the list of learning nuggets in your personal treasure chest.

"At the end of the quest, you will be able to reclaim ownership of your life. By doing so, you will help your wounded child to let go of the burdensome rocks in your backpack. As you become a master of change, you will find freedom from your past."

"I wish you could go with me, Jesse," Dakota said. "I trust you."

"I can't go with you because it is a personal quest, just as it was for me many years ago," Jesse explained. "You have to trust me on this one. There are people in Spain who will help you. They will provide you with money, transportation, and the necessary directions and documents you will need to move forward with your quest."

"You have gone on the same quest?" asked a surprised Dakota.

"Yes! That's why I'm so happy and content with my life," he answered. "And it's why I am so excited and eager for you to find happiness as well."

Jesse continued, "This trip will be an adventure, and you should pack accordingly.

There are a few items to carry with you at all times. You need to bring: An open mind to explore new ideas and possibilities, commitment, so you don't give up, perseverance and strength to overcome any obstacles, courage to be a risk taker, and a sense of humor"

Jesse put his hand on Dakota's shoulder, "Your adventure will not only be the most exciting trip you will ever take, but also the most important adventure of your life. This journey will present many challenges and pitfalls, but many treasures are waiting to be discovered!"

"When do I leave on this trip?" Dakota asked.

"Tomorrow," answered Jesse. "Your first destination is The City of the Past, located in Asturias on the north coast of Spain." Jesse handed Dakota a few brochures about the area, and Dakota placed them in his treasure chest.

"Asturias is a beautiful region of Spain," Jesse continued. "It's like a trip back in time. The region has some of the most beautiful rural scenery in all of Spain, with thousands of unexplored caves. It's a perfect place to discover what's in your backpack and reflect on your personal growth."

"How can I ever thank you, Jesse! I can't believe you've done all of this for me. I'm speechless."

Jesse again went inside the house and brought out a suitcase. He handed Dakota the luggage and told him, "Some of my friends and I pitched in to buy you this luggage along with some extra clothes and a good pair of hiking shoes. Luckily, I've been your mentor for all these years and I know your sizes.

"Well, Dakota, are you ready for the adventure of a lifetime?"

"Yes, sir!" said Dakota as he gave Jesse a warm hug. He tried to fight back the tears, but the emotions were too powerful.

"Thank you for being a part of my life and caring enough to give up your time to help me. Thank your friends for the luggage, shoes, and clothes."

"You're welcome," said Jesse. "I'll pick you up in the morning around 7:00."

"Goodnight," said Dakota. "Thanks again."

Dakota went through the luggage and added some of his favorite jeans and shirts. He packed his personal items in a sturdy duffel bag, along with the treasure chest. In his day pack, he placed a book that he hadn't had a chance to read, a journal that he had kept for a while, his passport, and his airline ticket.

Dakota's graduation day had been filled with many unexpected events and emotions. That morning, he'd had no idea that soon he would be on his way to Spain.

"I hardly know how to process this day," he thought. "You can certainly say I'm about to begin an adventure!"

Dakota closed his eyes and said a prayer of thanks.

CHAPTER TWO

CATERPILLARS & ELEPHANTS

This was Dakota's first airplane flight, and he was terrified and excited at the same time. "I'm buckled in and ready to go," he thought. From his window seat, he watched his home town disappear as the plane climbed into the clouds.

He leaned back in his seat when he heard the flight attendant ask, "Drinks or snacks?" Munching on crackers, he started to relax and read his book. He had read more than half of the pages before he fell asleep. The next thing he heard was the pilot's voice announcing that he was preparing to land. They had reached Spain!

After claiming his luggage, Dakota took a shuttle to his hotel. The City of the Past was about an hour from the airport, and Dakota was ready to enjoy the countryside. The scenery was breathtaking, with quaint stone cottages, rolling green hills, and spectacular mountains. The ride went by so quickly! The shuttle dropped everyone off, and the bellman helped Dakota with his luggage.

Before going to his room, Dakota stopped by the hotel gift shop, where he purchased several maps of the area. In his room, he quickly began to examine them.

"Hmm, I've been studying these maps for a while, but I haven't a clue where to start my quest. What do I do next? Where are the learning nuggets hidden? Where should I go to look for them?"

Just then, he heard a knock on the door. Opening it, Dakota saw a man and woman standing in the hall. The man reached out to shake Dakota's hand.

"Hello, Dakota," he said. "My name is Tony, and this is my wife, Rhonda. We've had a call from Jesse Patterson, and he asked us to help you begin your quest. We hope that's okay with you."

"Absolutely!" Dakota answered. "Please come in. I wasn't expecting you, but I'm glad you're here. I haven't a clue about what to do."

He felt better meeting these friends of Jesse. He knew he could trust them.

"It's such a beautiful day," Rhonda said. "Tony and I are going to take a hike in the countryside. Would you like to come with us, Dakota?"

"That's a great idea," Dakota answered. "We can get acquainted, and I'll have time to get my thoughts together."

The three new friends set out on their hike, and soon they were out in the fields and hills that surrounded the city.

"Oh, look. Dakota!" cried Rhonda. "There's a group of caterpillars inching their way around the base of a tree!"

"Oh, yes, I see them too," said Tony. "They are processionary caterpillars. There's something unique about that species."

"What is it" asked Dakota.

"Well," Tony began, "one processionary caterpillar will establish a direction, and all the others will fall in very closely behind and move in the same path. That's why they are called *processionary* caterpillars. A well-known French entomologist, Jean Henri Fabre, once led a group of these caterpillars onto the rim of a large flowerpot. The leader found itself nose to tail with the last caterpillar, forming a circle. What was interesting is that their natural habit and instinct prevented them from leaving the circle. The caterpillars circled the flowerpot for seven days and seven nights, until they died from exhaustion and starvation. The caterpillars continued to go around the flowerpot even though food was available, but simply outside their path."

"That's an interesting story," said Rhonda. "It must be hard for an individual caterpillar to know it is trapped in an endless circle. If you are walking around in a circle, there is no real starting point or a way to exit."

"Yes, that's right," Tony said. "All the processionary caterpillars were locked into their behavior and couldn't leave the circle. We humans are different from caterpillars because we have the ability to change the direction of our lives.

36

"The first step in creating change—a new path in life—is to become aware. Awareness lets us know there is a need for change and there may be a better way. How can you change what you are not aware of?

"The second step in creating change is to find the right knowledge. Knowledge allows problems to be solved and sometimes it lets us avoid them. If your car breaks down, mechanical knowledge is useful. It is the same with all of life's problems. We need to find the right knowledge to lead us out of the endless circle.

"The third step is to have the wisdom to use the right knowledge. Knowledge teaches us what we should do, wisdom is applying it effectively. We can have the knowledge that a steaming cup of coffee can burn us. Wisdom will use that knowledge to avoid getting burned."

Rhonda nodded in agreement. "If you want to step outside of the line to create a new path, you will need awareness, knowledge, and wisdom.

"Awareness is the ability to see other options. Knowledge gives us the facts and information to have a complete picture. Discernment gives us the ability to compare things to each other, but we need wisdom to understand the consequences of each.

Tony added to her comments, "You're standing at a crossroad and you have to decide between two paths. Discernment and wisdom will lead you to the best path."

Dakota couldn't wait to speak, "I got it! I saw a billboard in the city that read, 'In Awareness you will find knowledge and wisdom.' I saw an area called Awareness Park on my city map. That must be the starting point in my quest!"

Although the day had been sunny and warm, suddenly the wind turned cold and the sun disappeared behind dark storm clouds.

"It looks like a summer storm is blowing in," Tony said. "We don't have time to get back to the city before the rain starts."

Rhonda said, "I see a cave ahead. Let's run there. At least we can stay dry until the rain passes."

They gathered some wood as they ran across the field, and in just a few minutes Tony had built a small fire inside the cave. Rhonda brought out a bag of trail mix from her day pack, and they settled into their warm, cozy shelter.

As they sat around the fire, their talk turned to the importance of knowledge and wisdom. The more they talked, Dakota realized that many people are not aware of the difference between knowledge and wisdom, or that knowledge without wisdom is incomplete. To explain the difference, Tony told the story of six blind men and their experience when they met an elephant.

The Story of the Six Blind Men. [1]

Once upon a time in a faraway land, there lived six blind men. Each of them was very wise. Each of them had gone to school and read many books in Braille. They knew so much about so many things that people came from miles around to seek their advice. They were happy to share whatever they knew with the people who asked them thoughtful questions.

One day, these six wise blind men visited the zoo. It so happened that the zookeeper was worrying about her troubles that day. The night before, she'd had an argument with her husband, and her children had been misbehaving. She had so much on her mind that she forgot to lock the gate to the elephant enclosure as she was leaving it.

Now, elephants are naturally curious animals, and the leader of the elephants lumbered over to push the gate. To his great surprise, the gate swung open! The elephant looked left, looked right, and then quietly tiptoed through the gate to freedom.

At that very moment, the six blind men walked by. One of them heard a twig snap, and they all stopped to investigate what was ahead.

"Hi there!" said the first blind man to the elephant. "Could you please tell us the way to the zoo restaurant?"

The elephant couldn't think of anything intelligent to say, so he just shifted his weight from left to right and right to left.

The first blind man said, "I wonder whether this big silent person needs any help." Then, with a big bump, he walked right into the side of the elephant. He put out his arms to either side, but all he could feel was the elephant's huge body. "Wow!" said the blind man, "I think I must have walked into a wall."

The second blind man was becoming more and more curious about what was happening. He walked to the front of the elephant and grabbed the animal's trunk. He quickly let go and shouted, "This isn't a wall! This is a snake! Step back before it strikes!"

The third man decided to find out what was going on and tell his friends what they had encountered. He walked to the back of the elephant and touched the animal's tail. "This is no wall," he explained, "and this is no snake. You are both wrong. I know for sure that this is a rope."

The fourth blind man sighed. He knew how stubborn his friends could be. He decided that someone should really get to the bottom of this thing, so he crouched down on his hands and knees and felt around the elephant's legs. (Luckily for him, this elephant wouldn't think of stepping on a human being.) "My dear friends," explained the fourth man, "this is not a wall, and this is not a snake. This is not a rope, either. What we have here, gentlemen, are four tree trunks. That's it!—case closed."

The fifth blind man was not so quick to jump to conclusions. He walked to the front of the elephant and felt the animal's two long tusks. "It seems to me that this object is made up of two swords," he announced. "What I am holding is long and curved and sharp at the end. I am not sure what this could be, but maybe our sixth friend could help us."

The sixth blind man scratched his head and thought for a while. He was the wisest of them all. He was the one who really knew what he knew, and knew what he didn't know.

Just then, the worried zookeeper came by, looking for the wandering elephant. As she firmly grabbed the elephant's collar, she spoke to the six men.

"Hi, there! How are you enjoying the zoo today?" she asked.

"The zoo is very nice," replied the sixth blind man. "But my friends and I have a question that's puzzling us. Perhaps you could help us figure out what this thing is in front of us. One of us thinks it's a wall; one thinks it's a snake; one thinks it's a rope, one thinks it's four tree trunks, and one thinks it's two swords. How can one thing seem so different to five different people?"

"Well," said the zookeeper." This is an elephant. It seems like something different to each one of you. And the only way to know what it really is, is to do exactly what you have done. Only by sharing what each of you know can you possibly reach a true understanding."

The six wise men had to agree with the zookeeper's wisdom. The first five had been too quick to form an opinion without listening to what the others had to say. So they all went off to the zoo restaurant and enjoyed a hearty lunch. While they ate, they shared their unique thoughts with one other. Once they understood that it had been an elephant in front of them, they were able to have the complete picture.

Wisdom comes from knowing the whole elephant. Each blind man had a part of the whole picture. But without having all the facts, they continued to go in circles while defending their incomplete information.

"Like the blind men," Rhonda commented, "many of us have incomplete information based on our personal experiences. That information needs to be challenged if we want to create change. Dr. Phil McGraw tells us, "You can't change what you don't acknowledge."

Dakota agreed with Rhonda and pulled his journal from his day pack. "Excuse me for a minute," he said. "I want to make a few quick notes to myself in my journal."

JOURNAL

The elephant never changed. We go through life acting on our own perceived beliefs. The reason that people have so many different viewpoints is that we all get our knowledge from past experiences or from the experiences of others. When our knowledge is based on perception rather than reality, our decisions and behaviors will be affected. Awareness, knowledge, discernment, and wisdom will help to discover, what's in my backpack.

When Dakota had finished writing in his journal, Tony said, "The rain has stopped now. Let's head back to the city before dark."

They put out the fire and left the cozy cave, and soon they were back at Dakota's hotel. As they parted, Tony said, "Rhonda and I will take you to Awareness Park tomorrow. Goodnight!"

True to his word, the next morning Tony and Rhonda met Dakota soon after breakfast. The three friends left the hotel and walked a few blocks. As they walked, Rhonda told Dakota about the next mission in his journey.

"Many years ago, a monk wrote three scrolls on which he shared knowledge and wisdom with others. He hid the scrolls to protect them from those who didn't have the desire to apply the knowledge to their lives. You must find the scrolls. The knowledge written there will guide you in your quest for self-discovery. It will help you explore what has happened in your past and how the past has created who you are."

As they reached the end of the street, they found themselves at the entrance to a beautiful green fenced area. Over the entrance gate was a sign that read, "Welcome to Awareness Park."

"Here we are!" said Rhonda.

"We must leave you now," Tony said.

Dakota thanked Rhonda and Tony for their help and friendship. They said their goodbye, and Dakota entered through the gate to Awareness Park.

CHAPTER THREE

THE HIDDEN SCROLLS

Just inside the park entrance, Dakota saw a sign with arrows that directed visitors to two buildings. The arrow pointing to the north read, "The House of the Inner Garden," and the arrow pointing south read, "The House of Mysteries."

"I have a hunch I will find the scrolls within those two buildings," Dakota thought to himself. "I think I'll take the path to the inner garden first."

It didn't take long to locate the House of the Inner Garden. He entered the small building and discovered it held only one room with a few pieces of furniture. Everything looked unattended for a long time. He looked around, but he didn't see the scrolls. He tried to think like a monk. Where would he have hidden the scrolls?

Then his attention was drawn to an object that looked out of place. It appeared to be a large globe with a miniature garden within. Of course! He was in the House of the Inner Garden! Where would the Inner Garden scroll be hidden but somewhere near a garden!

Dakota turned the globe over and noticed that the base was larger than it should have been. A quick twist revealed everything. Hidden in the base of the globe was a parchment scroll!

He seated himself in a comfortable chair where a few rays of light illuminated the room. Carefully, as if the parchment might disintegrate at his very touch, Dakota unrolled the scroll and began to read the words that the monk had written so long ago.

Scroll I
The Inner Garden

There was a garden next to my hut. It had been unattended for many years, and it was full of weeds. I decided to turn that garden into something productive, something that I could be proud of. Since my garden had so many weeds, I decided to do small sections at a time so I wouldn't become overwhelmed and abandon the effort.

Picture in your mind a different kind of garden. Let's call it your inner garden. In this garden, we are not growing flowers but are cultivating and growing the inner self.

The mind and the garden work the same way.

James Allen, in his book, *As a Man Thinketh,* stated 'The mind, like a garden, can be intelligently cultivated or left unattended.'

If the garden is not cared for, unwanted seeds and then weeds will find their way into the soil and will continue to produce their own kind. "You reap what you sow" is true of your inner garden.

When a gardener plants an apple tree, he doesn't expect to harvest peaches. Nothing comes from apple trees but apples.

This truth applies to the inner garden as well. Nothing comes from positive but positive. If you plant goodness, you will harvest the results of goodness. If you plant love-centered beliefs, you will harvest love-centered results. When we plant seeds of fear, anger, resentment, self-pity, or disrespect for others, we will have unfavorable results.

Children do not know how to cultivate or care for their gardens. They are dependent upon others to do that for them. But as they grow older, they need to take ownership and responsibility for caring for their garden, even when it has been mismanaged by others. This is when the real life expedition begins. This is the greatest challenge of the expedition.

Everyone, no matter what age, needs to take ownership of their own property.

You are the only one who can manage your garden. No one can do it for you. If you do nothing, then unwanted weeds will continue to take over your garden and it will require a much greater effort to replace a field of weeds with productive plants.

Tending to your garden is not an easy task. It is a lifelong job.

Seek the next scrolls in the House of Mysteries.

Dakota thought about his early life and the monk's garden. He captured his thoughts in his journal.

JOURNAL

In the story of the inner garden, one's life is represented as a garden, and it's about taking ownership of who we are. Everything we do outwardly starts from within.

At some time in our life, we need to evaluate what is growing in our garden. As we begin to plant new thoughts and beliefs, we watch as they take root to bring forth new behaviors that are strong enough to bend but not break when the storms arrive. I remember a quote by Donna Kavanaugh, the author of The Garden: Our Inner Seasons of Planting and Growth. She wrote: 'We come to understand that the process of our inner gardening contains many miracles.'

Our faith grows when we begin to see the end results of our effort.

Dakota felt overwhelmed. There was so much information to absorb, and he felt some discomfort about visiting the past. "I have so much work to do on myself," he realized, "But for now, I will take one step at a time. I need to relax and put things aside for a while." He rolled the scroll and returned it to its place beneath the globe of the Inner Garden.

Dakota's mood lifted as he walked through the park on his way back to the hotel. A warm breeze blew gently, and birds were singing. He smiled and wondered what adventures and challenges were ahead tomorrow. Whatever the challenges might be, he knew he would be able to handle them.

The next morning, Dakota returned to the park and headed toward the House of Mysteries. Glancing around, he noticed a man he thought he had seen yesterday, but he stayed focused and was not deterred by his thoughts.

The building wasn't far from the park entrance, and he found it easily. As he approached, he observed that there were two doors to the building.

"Does it make a difference which door I enter first?" he wondered. "I guess the one on the left is where I'll start."

He found himself in a storage area lined with shelves and many books. "Looks like an old library," Dakota thought. All the books were well organized. He looked around for some clues as to where the next scroll might be, but he found none.

"Well, I'll try the other door and see what I can find in there," he decided.

He left the building and headed for the second door. "But wait!" he thought. "Is someone standing behind that tree?" He decided that his imagination was running away from him. Still, he hesitated for a moment before he opened the door and cautiously stepped inside.

In the dim light from a dirty skylight, he was amazed to see that the room was filled with small statues, each resting on its own pedestal. A chair and desk were the only furniture, and several lanterns hung on the wall. Reaching into his day pack, he took out a book of matches he had picked up at the hotel. He quickly lit each lantern, and the room was filled with sufficient light for him to see more clearly.

The statues all had a common theme—something to do with either the process of thinking or the awareness of the inner self.

Dakota started to inspect each statue, trying to find the scrolls. He carefully examined each statue, picking it up and searching its pedestal for a clue. About halfway through the collection, he was drawn to a statue on a stylish pedestal created with inset panels and trimmed beautifully with a decorative wood molding. On the pedestal was a replica of *The Thinker*, a sculpture by Auguste Rodin. The statue depicts a man who appears to be battling with internal struggles. Dakota saw an inscription below the statue: "The mind can process information at the speed of thought." He tried to pick up the statue, but found it was secured to its stand. When he rotated the statue, a drawer opened on the pedestal. Inside were two scrolls!

"Well, would you look at that!" he murmured.

He carefully picked up the scrolls and placed them on the desk. Not wanting to be interrupted while he read, he locked the door to outside.

He pulled the chair up to the desk. "I can't wait to read these messages," he said half-aloud as he unrolled the first scroll.

Scroll II
Mystery of the Two Minds

All of us are aware that we have a mind, but actually we have two separate minds working for us. The two minds are the conscious and subconscious. Understanding that each performs a different task is the key to unlocking the mystery.

The conscious mind is the thinker. It has the ability to reason and use logic. Think of the conscious mind as the programmer for the subconscious. It gathers all our past experiences and perceptions and sends them to the subconscious.

The subconscious, *like our backpack*, is the storeroom of our beliefs, memories, and skills. It is the sum total of all our past experiences. It is the home of our emotions—what we feel, think, and believe. Like a library, all perceptions and beliefs are stored in different categories that help create our habits and behaviors.

The subconscious doesn't have the ability to think or reason. It will always accept whatever is sent to it. It doesn't care whether the information is good or bad, true or false, nor does it care about the consequences. It just stores data and does it at the speed of thought. Information that has been accepted in the subconscious will remain until it is replaced by another belief.

The subconscious works on autopilot.

As babies, we don't know how to walk, so the conscious mind does all the reasoning so we can learn the skill of walking. At some point, the subconscious does it for us automatically with ease. We don't have to think about it. This is an example of how the two minds work together as a team. Whatever you want to achieve in life, the two minds must work together in harmony.

Be aware that the two minds can be in conflict. Emotions will often pit the conscious mind against the subconscious mind, thus creating conflict. It can be stated another way.

Whenever emotion and logic are in conflict, emotion usually wins. The more intense an emotion or experience, the deeper it is rooted in the subconscious. So the subconscious can have more influence on our actions than the conscious mind, but we usually are not aware of it.

Once, a little girl's mother told her not to get out of bed because a monster was hiding under there. Fifty years later, she still could not wait to get her feet off the floor as she got into bed. The conscious mind knew there wasn't a monster under her bed, but the embedded fear stored in the subconscious overruled the logical conscious mind.

The stronger the emotion that caused the belief, the more effort it requires for us to change that belief. This is another reason why change can be difficult.

The problem is, our subconscious will filter or reject information that isn't in harmony with its beliefs. If our beliefs are faulty, the decision making will be faulty.

We need to be aware of past conditioning and the effects it has on our future. There is a technique to train young elephants that clearly demonstrates the power of past conditioning. Let's investigate how you might train an elephant.

When the elephant is very young, the trainers tie a rope around its front leg and attach the rope to a peg in the ground. The elephant learns that when there is a rope on its leg, it cannot move. As the elephant gets older, the rope controls its movement even when the rope is no longer attached to the peg. At some point, the elephant never challenges that belief. Our belief system can be the rope that is holding us back.

Until the age of nine or ten, children's conscious minds are not fully developed. Until then, they don't have control over what is being stored or recorded in their subconscious. Therefore, children can fall victims to conditioning from others.

To be continued on Scroll III

Dakota placed the scroll on the desk and decided to take a break before reading the monk's next message. He was glad he had packed a bite to eat in his day pack. As he rested, he thought about the first scroll and the effect it had on him. He reached into his day pack, took out his journal, and started to write his thoughts.

JOURNAL

I remember a friend who aged out of foster care. His story is a good example of how emotions can overrule logic.

My friend told me about a period in his life when he was locked inside a room for a long time. Some twenty years later, he was sitting in a small commuter plane when he experienced claustrophobia. He began to feel trapped, and he desperately wanted to get out. He felt a lack of air, and he panicked.

Even though he had enough air and was safe, his environment triggered the subconscious to react emotionally. His mind accepted the fear as being real, so his emotions were real.

What caused him to have claustrophobia? It was past conditioning from his childhood, when he was locked in a room without any form of escape. Years later, he was still controlled by an event that happened when he was a child. That emotional event became deeply embedded in his subconscious, and logic couldn't overcome it.

I have never thought much about how the past could have such an effect on my life. I've mostly focused on things I could see—my outside world—and not my inner self.

Other people and past conditioning have played a big part in deciding who I am today. Understanding the mystery of the two minds gave me a crucial insight into my past. It has helped me evaluate who I am and how I became who I am today. I now have the knowledge to choose not to be a victim of the past. I can create my own path from this point forward.

Dakota always felt better after recording his thoughts in his journal. Writing down what he learned made him feel that he owned the new knowledge.

He closed his journal and left it on the desk. Eager to learn more, he unrolled the second scroll and began to read.

Scroll III
Mystery of the Two Minds

Dr. Maxwell Maltz, author of *Psycho-Cybernetics*, said that we have a built-in goal seeking "success mechanism" that is part of the subconscious mind. He goes on to explain the subconscious mind is always working to help us reach our potential.[1]

We activate our success mechanism by providing it with a clear target—a goal. If we fail to provide a clear target it will lie dormant. If you don't consciously choose to be drug free you may unconsciously begin to use. If you don't choose to eat healthy you may unconsciously become over weight. Other people may choose your goals if you don't. Peer pressure can be dangerous when we don't have clear goals.

Our subconscious wants to keep us safe, and usually it moves us toward what gives us satisfaction and away from what causes us pain. It does this by providing us with a comfort zone. We all have a comfort zone. As children, we find our comfort zone is like a rocking chair. It gives you something to do, but it doesn't get you anywhere.

We pretend to like where we are and who we have become, and therefore we want to stay there regardless of the consequences. This attitude can follow us into adulthood.

The danger is our comfort zone can interfere with our success mechanism. The reason for this is, our comfort zone is a safe place. It requires no effort or change because new experiences are uncomfortable, and usually we will do anything to avoid doing something different.

The comfort zone provides us with a set of limiting survival behaviors, which can include:

Fearing change and making mistakes

Sabotaging our efforts with negative self-talk

Being quick to create excuses or falling into victim behavior

Being overly concerned about what other people think

The only way to override limiting behaviors is to provide our subconscious with a new set of skills or instructions. We need to learn how to communicate to our subconscious in order to override the negative messages from our comfort zone.

Instructions will follow.

"Instructions will follow," Dakota repeated. "What a strange way for the monk to end his message! What in the world did he mean? Where are the instructions, and how will I find them?

"Well, it's been a long morning," he decided, "and I think I've had enough mystery for a while. I'll spend the afternoon here in Awareness Park. Perhaps after I rest, I'll be able to figure out what my next step will be."

He carefully rolled both scrolls, carried them to their pedestal, and placed them in the drawer. As he moved the statue of *The Thinker* back to its original position, the drawer silently slid shut, hiding its secret once more. Dakota unlocked the door and stepped outside into the bright afternoon sunlight.

In the distance, he caught a glimpse of trees and a small brook, and he headed in that direction. As he drew closer, he saw a tall tree that reminded him of his favorite tree back on the university campus. He ran toward it and settled himself under its outstretched branches. He sighed with the familiar "welcome home" feeling he'd always felt under his favorite tree, and be began to relax.

His thoughts returned to the scrolls. "Think of it! I've been reading ancient writings, and the message that worked way back then still applies to life today. We may all have different circumstances, but the message is the same for everyone.

"This would be a good time to record my thoughts about self-discovery," he decided. He brought out his journal from his day pack and began to write.

JOURNAL

Part of self-discovery is simply making a decision to no longer allow past conditioning from others to influence who I am or who I want to become. To break free, I will have to give my success mechanism clear goals and targets to reach. The opportunities for growth are endless.

Dakota read his journal entry. Satisfied with what he had written, he closed the journal and replaced it in his day pack.

Although he'd been alone just a few minutes earlier, now the park was bustling with activity. It was mid-afternoon, and groups of mothers were gathering on the park benches while their children played noisily on the broad lawns. Older kids whizzed by on their bicycles. A fruit vendor pushing an enormous wooden cart entered the park, weaving his way among the people and calling to them to come by his wares. Dakota's mouth began to water as he realized he had skipped lunch. He rose from his comfortable spot under the tree and walked across the lawn to meet the vendor. He selected a sandwich and a rosy apple from the tempting array on the cart and headed back to the tree to eat his lunch.

A young man came jogging up the path, a beautiful big black dog at his side keeping pace with its master. Just as they passed Dakota, the jogger reached out and pressed a slim book into Dakota's hands. "Here," the young man said, "I think you're expecting this." With that, he and his dog continued up the path.

Dakota glanced at the book title and almost fell to the ground in amazement. The book was titled, *Instruction Manual: Communicating With Your Subconscious Mind.*

"Wait!" Dakota called to the young man, but he and his dog had rounded a bend in the path and were out of sight.

All thoughts of hunger fled Dakota's mind as he retreated to the shade of his tree, settled himself against its broad trunk, and opened the book.

Instruction Manual:
Communicating With Your Subconscious Mind

A father bought a swing set for his children. He wanted to save time assembling it, and he didn't read the instructions, instead relying on his own instincts. Not only were the final results wrong, the swing set was unsafe. The end results were lost time, confusion, and stress. Finally, the father read the instructions and followed each step. Life is not enjoyable if you are getting the wrong instructions. Think about it!

Like the swing set story, instructions for reprogramming your subconscious mind must be read, understood, and applied to get the results you desire.

If you want to change how you live your life and reach your goals, give your subconscious a new set of instructions. Skills that will help make it happen include desire, repetition, affirmations, and visualization.

Desire

The stronger the desire to learn something new, the faster the change will occur. The desire for the new habit must be stronger than the desire for the old habit.

There is a story about Jacob and his sister Rachel. As youngsters, they loved to swim in a nearby river. One day while swimming, Jacob and Rachel were having fun dunking each other. Rachel didn't realize it, but she had moved into deeper water and her feet could no longer touch the bottom of the river. Jacob started to dunk her again and again, but now her feet didn't have the support to push herself upward. She couldn't breathe, and she was terrified. She wanted nothing else but air. When you want to change as much as Rachel wanted air, then you'll be ready for change.

Repetition

Habits are created by repetition. Behaviors can become habits only through repetition. The more passionate you are about the change, the more effective the repetitions will be as you begin to reprogram the subconscious mind.

Dr. Maxwell Maltz, a plastic surgeon and the author of the bestseller, *Psycho-Cybernetics,* noticed that it took 21 days for amputees to stop feeling phantom sensations in the area of the amputation. With further observations, he discovered it took 21 days to create a new habit. The 21-day habit theory has become an accepted part of self-help programs.

Dakota remembered a story that supports the theory: A man noticed that a gas station was offering free coffee for a month to celebrate its grand opening. He decided to take advantage of the offer. After a month, where do you think he stopped to get his coffee and fill his tank with gas? Yes, he continued to go to the new gas station. He had developed a new habit.

Reading your goals each day is also a form of repetition. Write them down and place them where you can see them and read them every day. Also, the more you speak your goal verbally, or the more you talk about it, the stronger you will believe it. Read It, Think It and Say It.

Remember, the subconscious will accept whatever it is told—so don't quit practicing the new habit until you are able to do it without thinking about it.

Affirmations

An affirmation is a statement that we acknowledge to be true. Your subconscious works in harmony with your beliefs and will make a case for it. If you say, "I can't," your subconscious will remind you of all the reasons why you can't.

Affirmation is about listening to our self-talk and erasing negative messages we send to ourselves. Negative self-talk is a hurdle to personal growth and a roadblock that prevents us from reaching our goals. Positive self-talk is about believing in ourselves and building self-confidence.

Whether the affirmations are negative or positive, they work equally either for or against you. Negative affirmations include:

I can't—What if—It won't work—I'm stupid—I'm ugly—I'm fat.

Pay attention to your self-talk and make a conscious effort to manage it.

Visualization

You have probably heard the expression, "You are what you think." Visualization is the process of creating mental pictures. It's a way of thinking without using words. You can use your imagination to help you reach your goal by overcoming limited thinking.

The power of visualization was illustrated in a study conducted by Dr. Blaslotto at the University of Chicago. The goal was to determine the effects of visualization on performance.

He divided the students into three groups and their ability to shoot baskets was recorded. The first group was excluded from the basketball court for 30 days. The second group was allowed to practice every day for one hour. The third group was only allowed to imagine shooting baskets for an hour each day.

At the end of 30 days, there were some fascinating results. As you would expect, Group one, who had not practiced at all, had made no improvement. Group two, who had practiced daily, recorded a 24% improvement. Group three, who only imagined shooting baskets, had improved their performance by 23%! This was almost the same improvement as the group who had actually practiced. The subconscious doesn't distinguish between an actual event and a vividly imagined one. Change the way you communicate with your subconscious mind. See it, feel it, say it, and believe it!

Dakota took a deep breath. The messages in the scrolls and the instruction manual had given him hope for the future. He began to think about how important it is to have the right instructions.

Computers, play stations, and iPods all come with instructions. If we choose not to read the instructions and just wing it, our new electronic device will start, but it may not give us all its features and benefits. Our learning may be hit-and-miss. Reading the instructions will produce results much faster and can even prevent damage.

Dakota began to realize that it was getting late. The park was almost empty and the sun was setting. It was time to return to his hotel.

Entering his room, Dakota saw that someone had slipped an envelope under his door. He opened the envelope and took out a note:

You have finished your quest here in The City of the Past. Make a list of the learning nuggets you have gathered here. At 7:00 tomorrow morning, a driver will take you to the airport. Give your list to the gatekeeper. He will provide you with an airline ticket. The next leg of your expedition will take you to The Village of Principles. We hope you have enjoyed your stay here, but you cannot return once you leave. Keep the Instruction Manual with you throughout your life. The learning nuggets will be useless without having the right instructions.

Dakota pondered the knowledge he had gained over the past two days. He was aware that it would change his life. Each learning nugget was a piece of the puzzle that had to be put together so his wounded child would understand how it would affect his future.

Early the next morning, Dakota prepared his checklist for the gatekeeper.

The Learning Nuggets Checklist

• Awareness, knowledge, discernment, and wisdom are the starting points to create change.
• Discernment gives us the ability us to compare things to each other, but we need wisdom to understand the consequences of each.
• The mind and the garden work the same way. Everything we do outwardly starts from within. Nothing comes from apple trees but apples.
• Ownership means that I am the only one who can manage my garden.
• We all are governed by two minds: the conscious and the subconscious.
• The future can be influenced by past experiences, past conditioning, and programming from others. This is why children can fall victims to faulty programming.
• If the data is faulty, the decisions will be faulty.
• When we have two conflicting beliefs, one based on logic and the other based on emotions, the one based on emotions will almost always win.
• Each of us has a built-in goal-seeking "success mechanism" that requires a clear target.
• It takes 21 days to create a new habit.
• The subconscious needs the right instruction to override the negative messages from our comfort zone. Desire it, Practice it, Say it, See it, and Feel it.

After breakfast, Dakota went to the front desk to meet his driver. As he entered the lobby, he had a distinct feeling that someone was following him. He dropped the thought when his driver approached.

"Good morning Mr. Stone. I'm here to take you to the airport."

They loaded Dakota's luggage and headed for the city gate. On the way, Dakota noticed a vehicle that he thought he had seen before.

"Do you think that car behind is following us?" Dakota asked the driver.

"Let's see," replied the driver. He made a left turn and then a right. The car was still behind them, but a little farther back.

"I think you're right," the driver said. "I'd better let the gatekeeper know we're being followed."

"That might be a good idea," Dakota agreed.

A few minutes later, they slowly pulled up to the gatekeeper's station.

"Hello, Charlie," said the driver. "We seem to have a problem. We're being followed by the car behind us."

Charlie glanced at the next car. "I'll handle it," he said.

Dakota sighed with relief and handed him the checklist.

Charlie read Dakota's list and smiled. "Congratulations, my friend. You have made great progress and acquired much knowledge here in The City of the Past."

"Yes, I have," Dakota replied. "Now I understand that wisdom comes from knowing how to use knowledge, and by applying wisdom I can achieve a better life."

"It sounds like you're ready for the next phase of your quest," said Charlie.

"Yes, sir! I am," answered Dakota.

Charlie handed the checklist to Dakota, who placed it in his treasure chest. Then the gatekeeper gave him an envelope containing an airline ticket.

"Your next stop will be the Kalahari Desert in Botswana, Africa. There you will meet your guide.

"Good luck and God Bless!" Charlie waved as they drove away.

When the next car approached the gate, Charlie pretended to find a problem with their documents. He detained them long enough for Dakota to be safely on his way.

SELF-EMPOWERMENT
WHAT ARE YOU ROOTED IN?

CHAPTER FOUR

THE CAVE OF RUNNING WATERS

The flight from Spain to the Kalahari Desert in Africa was not exactly the "friendly skies." To conserve funds, Dakota was given the lowest-cost ticket available. Little did he know that he would be sharing accommodations with men and animals! They both smelled the same.

The plane made a rough landing at a small airstrip in northern Botswana. A few men and camels were waiting for Dakota when he exited the plane.

The group was led by a tall, muscular man named Akua. He had lived in Zimbabwe all of his life, and his vast knowledge of the region and Botswana's fragile ecosystem made him a valuable professional guide. Akua welcomed Dakota to south-central Africa. "Please leave your luggage. It will be at your hotel when you arrive tonight," he promised.

"Are you sure?" Dakota asked.

"I don't think your camel wants to carry you *and* your luggage," laughed Akua.

Dakota laughed with him. "Is it okay to take my day pack?"

"No problem," responded Akua. "We have a two-hour trip to the Chobe River. Once we reach the river, a boat will take us to the Zambezi River. From there, we will go to Victoria Falls in Zambia."

"Is that the famous Victoria Falls you are talking about?" asked Dakota.

"Yes" Akua replied. "Victoria Falls is the largest waterfall in the world, and one of the Seven Wonders of the World."

"Wow!" said Dakota. "That's awesome!"

"We will dock just before reaching the falls," Akua continued. "From there, we will take a jeep to The Village of Principles in Zimbabwe."

He handed Dakota an African safari hat to protect his head and face from the sun.

"Have you ever mounted a camel?" he asked.

"No, sir," Dakota replied.

"Okay. First," Akua explained, "always mount the camel while it is down on all fours. Get one foot into the stirrup, and throw the other leg over the camel's hump. Maintain a good posture to prevent rolling to either side. Hold your reins confidently. A camel can sense if you're nervous. And always dismount the camel when it is on all fours again."

"I can handle that." said Dakota confidently.

They traveled across impressive sand dunes, some as high as 200 feet. Shimmering waves of heat rose from the desert floor, revealing an amazing spectrum of color—every shade of brown to beige, red, even white in some areas. Dakota couldn't believe he was trekking across the desert on a camel's back! Without a doubt, this was one of the most exciting things he had ever done—but not the most comfortable. Nevertheless, he felt at peace as the camel's rhythmic gait gently rocked him back and forth.

They passed through a surprising patch of tangled green vines, and Dakota called out, "Look, Akua! Are those *watermelons* growing wild in the sand?"

"Yes," Akua replied. "Watermelons originated in the Kalahari Desert. In this intense heat, the natives quench their thirst on the sweet fruit."

As they reached the far edge of the desert, they dismounted their camels and transferred to a jeep waiting to take them to the river. Between desert and river, the terrain changed dramatically. They drove through dense forests, plunging ravines, and lush savanna grasslands.

"You are in for a treat," Akua said. "The Zambezi and Chobe rivers form one of the most productive natural ecosystems on the continent.

"The Chobe River flows along the northern border of Chobe National Park. The park is famous for its abundance of wildlife, and some 60,000 elephants roam through the park. Other animals that live here are leopards, cheetahs, giraffe, kudu, and wildebeest.

"As we travel the river, you may see hippos, crocodiles, and otter. Watch the river banks for herds of buffalo and zebra. The river attracts over 400 different species of birds."

As they passed through the grasslands, Akua pointed to a pride of lions sleeping away the afternoon. Dakota was beginning to understand just how much Akua loved this magnificent land.

"Are you going to continue with me all the way to Zimbabwe?" Dakota wondered.

Akua assured him that it was his job to make sure Dakota would arrive safely in Zimbabwe. "There is a customs and immigration station ahead," said Akua. "Let me do the talking. If anyone says anything to you, just tell them I'm your tour guide."

"Okay—but are we in any danger?"

"I'm not sure," Akua replied. "Just do as I say."

Their pass through the customs station went smoothly, but Dakota was aware that Akua cautiously hurried him aboard the double-decker boat to Victoria Falls.

"Let's get something to eat and sit on the top deck," Akua said.

As they ate, Akua told Dakota. "I think we're being followed." He nodded to a much smaller boat behind them.

"Why are they following us?" Dakota asked.

"A small military group from The City of the Past is opposed to our beliefs. They are afraid that when people learn the truth about self-discovery, they will rebel. They want to destroy your treasure chest that holds the nuggets checklist and instruction manual before others can read them. Here in Africa, they also have support from a local group that shares their beliefs."

"What should we do?" asked Dakota.

"We can try to ditch them when we dock in Zambia, but we'll have to move quickly," Akua answered. He handed Dakota a bag with tourist-type clothing. "We will change into our traveling clothes just before we're ready to get off the boat. We'll reach our drop-off in about an hour. In the meantime, relax and enjoy the view."

Dakota wondered how he could relax while people were following them, but he did try. Surprisingly, he found himself forgetting his fears as he watched a group of elephants guarding their young, and along the shore zebras nervously drank from the river as the boat passed by.

Just before the boat docked, Dakota and Akua changed their clothes. They were the first ones off the boat and quickly jumped into a waiting jeep.

"I think we lost them," Akua smiled.

"Okay!" Dakota exclaimed, giving Akua a high-five. "Now I can relax and get a better look at the falls!"

Akua told Dakota, "The river forms the border between Zambia and Zimbabwe. Victoria Falls Bridge crosses the Zambezi River and is built over the second gorge of the falls. There you can get a good view. But we can't linger at the falls. We have to keep moving."

"I understand completely," Dakota responded.

The view of the falls was indeed spectacular, but Akua's constant backward glances reminded Dakota that they still might be in danger.

"At the end of the bridge there is a border post," Akua said. "Again, let me do the talking."

Dakota was happy as they crossed the border without incident.

As they drove away, Akua told Dakota, "There is an old folktale about a wise man named Uni. Many claim that he doesn't exist, but others believe he does. Those who do believe say he is a hermit who appears in a cave when someone seeks his wisdom and knowledge. He is said to have valuable information about universal principles. Those who seek him believe he is kind and warm-hearted. To many, he represents a father. When no one is seeking his advice, he finds peace living and studying with the monks at a nearby monastery."

Dakota suspected that the universal principles might be the next learning nugget he needed to understand. If that were so, his next mission would be to find Uni—if Uni even existed.

"Can you take me to Uni?" Dakota asked.

"Sorry," Akua answered. "Uba is the better person to help you find Uni. I have hired Uba as a guide many times, and he has told me that

Uni does exist. Uba lives just outside The Village of Principles. We should arrive there soon. I will take you to meet him."

It didn't take long for Akua to find Uba's home. When Dakota explained to Uba that he wanted to meet Uni, Uba shook his head. "No," he said firmly. Like his father and grandfather before him, Uba felt a solemn obligation to protect Uni and the location of his cave.

Dakota didn't accept his refusal. He pleaded with Uba to take him to Uni.

"What is your purpose for wanting to visit Uni?" Uba asked.

"I want to understand the mystery of universal principles," Dakota answered.

That simple statement seemed to soften Uba's heart. He was silent for a few minutes before he agreed to be Dakota's guide.

"Where can we find this legend?" asked Dakota.

"We will travel to Zimbabwe's eastern highlands." Uba pointed to the area. "There we will find him in a cave near Mutarazi Falls. We will leave at daybreak."

As Dakota headed toward the jeep, Uba handed him a map to examine.

By the time they arrived at The Village of Principles, Dakota was exhausted. When he entered his room at the lodge, he was surprised to see his luggage. He had totally forgotten about it.

A hot shower and dinner were on the top of his list. He was amazed at how comfortable his room was, and the dinner was delicious.

In The Village of Principles, the people were calm and happy. Could their behavior be the result of living by principles? Dakota thought about how different the village was, compared to The City of the Past, where people seemed to be traveling endlessly in circles.

Dakota studied the map that Uba had given him. "This will be a difficult journey," he realized. They would travel sandy roads, unmarked trails, and steep inclines, not to mention perhaps encountering snakes and wild animals. He felt a shiver of uneasiness— he hated snakes!

Dakota awoke well before daybreak, dressed quickly, and ate breakfast at the lodge. He decided to wait outside for Uba. A small dust devil whipped around him, and again he wondered how difficult the trip might be.

Uba showed up just before dawn. He loaded the jeep, started the engine, and the two men drove out of the village as the sun rose over the horizon.

After three hours of heat and dust, the primitive road came to an end.

"The rest of the journey will be on foot," Uba explained.

They moved the jeep to a secluded spot and covered it with large branches and grass, and then gathered their equipment and headed toward the mountains.

"With luck, we should arrive at the cave before dusk," said Uba. "There we will make camp for the night."

Uba used his native skills to navigate the rough unmarked trail. Amazed, Dakota followed close behind.

"FREEZE!" shouted Uba. "Don't move!" In a hollow tree to the left of Dakota, a snake hissed its presence. Dakota froze, his eyes following the hissing snake poised to strike. With everything inside telling him to run, he remained still. His heart was beating so hard he thought he would faint. Finally, the snake slowly and silently slithered away.

"Wow! That was close!" Dakota breathed as his heartbeat returned to normal.

"That was a Black Mambas, one of Africa's most dangerous and feared snakes," Uba informed him. "Let's keep moving before it gets dark and you have something much bigger to fear," Uba teased.

"Ha-ha!" Dakota joined Uba's laughter. "I can keep up with you."

Dakota was happy that they arrived safely at Uni's cave just as light was fading. They quickly set up camp and started a fire. Uba's crafty hunting skills provided local game for dinner. After they had eaten, Dakota pulled his bedroll close to the fire, and soon both men were fast asleep.

In the morning, Dakota was awakened by the aroma of fresh coffee. Uba greeted him and explained that he would go no farther.

"The journey to Uni is a personal journey best taken alone," he said reverently.

He pointed to the mouth of the cave. "Enter there," he said. "Follow the stream. It will lead you to Uni. I will remain here and will take you back to the village."

Dakota thanked Uba and entered the cave. The cool, damp air was refreshing, as was the faint sound of a waterfall. As he walked farther into the cave, the sound became louder, and Dakota knew he was close to Uni's shelter. He wondered what Uni would look like and how he would act.

He turned a bend in the stream and reached the falls. What a magical place! Sunlight streamed through an opening at the top of the cave. It lit up the waterfall and created a beautiful rainbow. Imagine!—a rainbow in a cave!

He looked around, but found no one. He started to wonder whether Uni was just a legend after all. But just then, an ancient man appeared from behind the falls. His hair was long, and he had a well-trimmed beard. His voice was gentle as he greeted Dakota. "I have been waiting for you," he said. "Please come into my shelter. Sit with me by the fire."

"Wow!" Dakota thought, as he sat across from Uni by the cozy fire. "This is my time to soak up Uni's knowledge and wisdom!"

Uni asked gently, "Why have you come here, Dakota?"

"I want to understand the universal principles," Dakota answered.

Uni began to explain, "Have you ever thought about what the world would be like without gravity? There definitely would be disorder. Just as gravity helps the world to function in harmony, principles bring harmony to our lives. And as the world is governed by universal laws, our lives are governed by universal principles. Without principles, there would be chaos in our lives."

"Why are they called universal?"

Uni smiled. He was pleased that Dakota was so eager to learn.

"Principles are called universal because they apply to all generations. They have been passed down through the ages. Principles have been the same since I was a young man, and even when Moses was a young man. However, your understanding of them can have a tremendous effect on your life.

"Look at principles as an internal compass that guides us. Navigators depend on the compass to determine true north, choices that are aligned with principles become your true north. Values and principles define how we lead our lives and our character is a reflection of them.

Bill George in his book, True North, stated: 'It is easy to drift off course as the temptations and pressures of daily life pull you away from doing the right thing. It is your values and principles that draw you back, enabling you to perform in an ethical manner.'

So, do not believe that your work is done until you have wisely chosen your principles."

Dakota said, "I never gave much thought to principles before. How do principles affect how I live my life?"

"Good question," Uni answered. "Let's examine how principles apply to character. The strength and flexibility of a building starts in its foundation. The strength of our character is built on the foundation of principles. Your character is shaped by what you do, and every choice you make defines the kind of person you will become.

"No one can give you character—it's a choice. Once you develop character, no one can take it away from you.

"You can think of people with good character as being action driven. Action driven principles create action-driven people. Action-driven people are in gear and on the move. They take ownership for what they do and who they are. They avoid neutral, because in neutral they are either standing still or coasting downhill.

"When confronted with a choice, ask yourself, if this choice violates any action-driven principles, and what are the consequences of this choice?

"Your mission here is to find the key principles that build character.

"Let me give you an easy way to remember some key principles," Uni continued. "They are the:

Three R's, (Responsibility, Respect for self, and Respect for others.)
Three C's, (Courage, Caring, and Community service.)
Good judgment, (Choose friends carefully, Be fair minded and Obey all laws and rules.)"

As Uni talked about principles, Dakota made notes in his journal.

JOURNAL

Responsibility

Be accountable for your actions.
Think before you act and consider the consequences.
Do what you have to do, before you do what you want to do.
Have a good attitude.
Be positive and know you can handle whatever happens.
Be cheerful and have a sense of humor.
Be flexible. Don't get stressed out over things you can't control.
Be trustworthy.
Be dependable and reliable. Do what you say. Keep promises.
Don't cheat, lie, or steal.

Respect for Self

Be true to yourself.
Don't compare yourself to others or belittle yourself.
Do the right thing, even when others around you are not.
Value your strength and acknowledge your weaknesses.
Take care of your body.
Practice cleanliness. Eat healthy food. Exercise regularly.
Avoid substance abuse and unplanned pregnancy.

Respect for Others

Treat others as you want to be treated.
Treat all people as individuals regardless of race, religion, age, and gender.
Solve problems without violence and hostility.
Be courteous and polite.
Say please, thank you, and you're welcome.
Hold open a door. Don't cut in line. Watch your language.
Honor the property of others.

Courage

Do the right thing, even when no one is watching.
Admit when you're wrong.
Apologize early and gracefully.
Ask for help.

Don't worry about what people might think.
Don't act on impulse, manage your emotions.
Accept honest criticism, discipline, and instruction.

Caring
With action.
Help others in need and do small acts of kindness.
Don't hold grudges. Forgive yourself and others for mistakes.
Focus on good and not the bad.
With words.
Use kind words of praise, instead criticism.
Avoid gossip and rumors.
Speak in a kind voice when you disagree with others.

Community Service
Volunteer.
Recycle.
Create a strong family environment.
Pass on family heritage, culture and traditions.
Develop spirituality

Good Judgment
Choose friends carefully.
You become who you hang around with.
Be fair-minded.
Be impartial, reasonable and fair. Listen to others.
Obey all laws, and rules.
Freedom without rules, creates chaos.

Uni continued to explain, "Action-driven principles are not rules to follow but choices to decide who you want to be. Let each principle challenge you to create your own inner garden and independence.

"When you live by action driven principles, people will trust and depend on you and enjoy being with you. People with good character are honest, respectful, reliable, and responsible.

"How much character would a young man have if he promised to mow the lawn and didn't do it? What if he promised not to do drugs, but when he felt pressured by others he did it anyway? Think about a woman who tells a secret she had promised to keep. What if someone lied and deceived you and you forgave that person, who then did it again. Would you trust or depend on that relationship? Would you believe that person has good character?

"A friend agreed to help you set up a special event, but didn't show up. Can you trust or depend on that person? Being trustworthy is one trait of a person with good character.

"Honesty and integrity go hand in hand. Honesty is, simply, the lack of intent to deceive. All types of evasion are deceitful. When you stop deceiving yourself and others, you open the door to total honesty.

"People with integrity don't compromise their principles and character. Two efforts that will fail are to behave exactly the way someone else wants you to behave or to get others to behave the way you want them to."

Dakota said, "I'm getting the point, and I'm starting to see some flaws in my character that I need to correct. You are teaching me that my internal compass is my personal road map to becoming productive and happy. The key is to take ownership for the development of my internal compass. Action driven principles are the true north to guide me in the right direction. My compass shows me the direction, and I need to focus on staying on the right course."

Uni nodded in agreement. "I'm impressed by your honesty," he said. "It takes courage to admit one's flaws."

Uni asked Dakota to listen to the story of two Olympic skaters and identify the missing principles.

"Nancy Kerrigan was favored to win the 1994 U.S. Figure Skating Championship. Tonya Harding, a 1991 champion, and her husband knew that if Kerrigan was out of the competition, it would improve Tonya's chances of winning.

"Nancy Kerrigan was attacked with a metal baton on the upper left knee as she left the ice after a practice session. She had to withdraw from the competition. Tonya knew the truth of what happened to Kerrigan, but she kept silent. In Kerrigan's absence, Harding captured the spotlight—but not for long. She would pay a heavy price. She lacked the valuable principles of integrity, honesty, and respect. Harding's weak character was devastating to her career. If only she had aligned her values with principles, her life would have taken a different turn. One of her last public appearances was on a pay-per-view female boxing event. What a sad ending for a graceful and talented skater."

Uni continued, "Self-respect isn't about getting approval from others or cheating your way into the spotlight. It does mean that you embrace your own self-worth and dignity, and you feel comfortable with both your strengths and your weaknesses. It's about knowing your limitations and being comfortable with them. You may want to be a rock star, but if you can't carry a tune, you need to move on. When you have a healthy self-respect, you will not be damaged by the limits of your talents or threatened by the talents of others."

Uni went on to explain another important key principle—love.

"Love is one of my favorite principles," he said. "You can love many people at the same time—a friend, your family, your pet, or even your car. I love this cave." He smiled as he glanced around his shelter.

"Anyone can say, 'I love you.' A husband might hit his spouse or children and later say, 'I love you.' A mother may be verbally abusive, but later say, 'I love you.' Saying the words, 'I love you' is easy, but the quality of your love is more important than mere words. Actions must support the words. When love is based on action driven principles, it not only improves your relationships, it also improves the quality of your life.

"Let's focus on the main ingredients we need to create a loving relationship. I'll compare it to baking a cake. What would happen if you left out the flour, a main ingredient? Now take out the eggs. What would happen to your cake?

"What would happen to a relationship if you left out the main ingredients of honesty, respect, and appreciation? Never leave out a dash of forgiveness. The truth is, none of us is perfect, so sometimes we mess up and need to be forgiven. What happens when you leave out accountability? You end up with a controlling behavior, and controlling behaviors are not aligned with action driven principles.

"A controlling person will use guilt, anger, and rejection to punish and control others. Stephen R Covey said it best: 'You can't talk your way out of what you've behaved yourself into.'

"Another way to define love is, a lack of preoccupation with self. Two self-centered words are: 'I' and 'me.' 'You are doing it to me.' 'If only you would change, I would be happy.' 'After all I did for you— you don't love or appreciate me.' Love is a choice, and we decide every day how to communicate that love."

With that, Uni rose and left the cozy warmth of the fire. "That is enough for now," he told Dakota. "It is time for you to continue your quest. There is much more that you need to discover. I have not shared all the principles. Life has a way of leading you to the other principles when the time is right. I encourage you to keep your eyes focused on the future. Always remember, you can't have a new beginning, but you can create a new ending."

Uni led the way back to the stream. As they walked, Uni said, "The next part of your journey will take you to Blue Mountain, an area near Sydney, Australia. There you will find two time zones. In the west is the Land of Pause, and to the east is Nowhere Land. You will be staying in the village of Truth or Consequences, located between these lands. Your mission is twofold—to understand which zone offers a better way of life, and to determine what kind of person you want to become."

They reached the waterfall, and Dakota knew that Uni would walk with him no farther. He felt sad to leave Uni, and he understood why he was considered a wise and gentle father.

Uni embraced Dakota with a warm hug. "Bon voyage, my friend," he said.

Dakota's voice was choked with emotion as he thanked Uni. "I'll never forget this day," he managed to say. Uni gave a little wave and disappeared behind the waterfall.

Outside the cave, Uba was waiting. "Have you found what you were seeking?" he asked.

Dakota smiled. "More than I hoped for," he answered.

Uba brought Dakota to the camp. "We will stay here tonight and leave at daybreak," he said.

The next morning, Uba woke Dakota with fresh coffee and a warm breakfast. "It will be another long day," he told Dakota. "We will reach the village at nightfall."

"How lucky I am to have Uni as my mentor," Dakota realized. "I wonder whether there will be a mentor waiting for me in Australia."

Just as Uba had predicted, they arrived at the village as the sun was setting. Dakota paid Uba and thanked him for getting him home safely.

"No problem, my friend. You take care and watch out for those snakes!" Uba chuckled.

After the long day in the heat and dust, Dakota showered and had dinner in his room. He didn't sleep well that night. He had too many thoughts about implementing all that he had learned from Uni.

In the morning, he prepared his list for the gatekeeper.

The Learning Nuggets Checklist

- Principles are universal. They do not change with the passing of time.
- Principles are an internal compass that guides us.
- Values and principles define how we lead our lives and our choices are a reflection of our principles and values.
- Action-driven principles are the foundation for building good character.
- We're not born with character. We can develop character.
- Action-driven principles create action-driven people.
- I will filter my choices through action-driven principles.
- Love is a choice. We decide every day how to express love to each other.
- Never use guilt, anger, or rejection to punish or control others.
- Controlling behaviors are not an expression of love.
- There are many principles that create a loving, quality relationship.

Dakota asked one of the drivers at the lodge to take him to the airport. At the city gate, he handed his checklist to the gatekeeper. After reading the list, the gatekeeper gave it back, and Dakota carefully placed it in his treasure chest.

"I see you have spent your time wisely while visiting our village," said the gatekeeper. "Your nugget list is impressive!" He handed Dakota a sealed envelope containing an airline ticket.

"Please come back to visit again," said the gatekeeper.

As he drove away, Dakota murmured, "Yes, I will be back."

CHAPTER FIVE

BLUE MOUNTAIN

The sixteen-hour flight from Zimbabwe to Sydney, Australia, left Dakota well rested, but the eight-hour difference in time zones really confused his body clock.

During the flight, Dakota had quiet time to think about his quest. "I'm beginning to realize that life isn't an escape—you can't run from your past, you can only embrace it. I like the idea of being an action-driven person. Regardless of my past, I can create a better me. Uni told me, 'You can't have a new beginning, but you can create a new ending.' I have begun to create that new ending."

The plane was starting its descent, and Dakota glanced out the window. "Wow! That must be Blue Mountain." The view was breathtaking! Towering cliffs, deep ravines, and impressive gorges held him spellbound until the view disappeared and the plane landed.

While waiting for his luggage, Dakota picked up a few brochures. One was about the ZigZag Railway, built right up the face of a cliff. He loved trains! He hoped he would have time to ride the ZigZag or visit the Three Sisters, a famous rock formation located nearby.

After he claimed his luggage, he boarded a shuttle bus to his hotel in the village of Truth or Consequences. As the bus arrived at his hotel, Dakota wondered whether this place would have the same effect on him as he had experienced at the Village of Principles.

The desk clerk greeted him. "Welcome to Blue Mountain, Mr. Stone. I see this is your first visit to the area. Our guest coordinator, Miss Jones, will explain why you were sent to Blue Mountain. She will answer your questions and make your stay a comfortable one. Miss Jones will be in touch with you shortly. Please remain in your room until she contacts you."

He handed the room key to the bellman, and the bellman gathered Dakota's belongs. The room was furnished simply, with a desk, a comfortable chair, and a soft bed. Dakota was about to unpack when he heard a knock at the door. A young woman stepped into the room.

"Hello, Mr. Stone, I'm Miss Jones, your guest coordinator. Welcome to our village."

Dakota had not given much thought to what Miss Jones might look like, but that all changed—he was instantly attracted to her. He thought to himself, "How beautiful she is!"

"Hello, Miss Jones. I've been waiting for you."

"My friends call me Sunshine," she smiled.

"And my friends call me Dakota," he laughed.

Sunshine asked, "Do you have your treasure chest and instruction manual with you?"

"Yes, I do."

"I suggest you lock them and any other valuables in the room safe."

"I absolutely understand. I have already encountered people who wanted to steal them."

Sunshine continued, "The village of Truth or Consequence lies between the Land of Pause and Nowhere Land. The mountains, with their laid-back atmosphere and unspoiled beauty, offer a peaceful place to reflect on life. I like to think of our village as a stepping stone to taking back the ownership of your life. You can achieve this through self-empowerment."

Dakota asked, "What do you mean by self-empowerment?"

"That's a good question," she answered. "Self-empowerment is the process of taking control of your choices and understanding their consequences. It is the way you choose to conduct yourself.

"Now that you have a better understanding of self-empowerment," Sunshine said, "you have three important goals to accomplish here at Blue Mountain.

"Your first goal is to understand what you can control and what you can't control.

"Your second goal is to decide which kind of person you want to be—a chooser or a loser.

"Your third challenge will be to investigate the two nearby zones—the Land of Pause and Nowhere Land—and decide which behavior zone you will use to manage your life. The Land of Pause is an uncharted territory that offers new insights. Nowhere Land is a more familiar zone—a comfort zone.

"This part of your quest will start at the library in the center of the village. I will give you a riddle. When you have solved it, tell your answer to the librarian. If you have the right answer, she will give you the key to a special room. There you will find the way to self-empowerment.

"Be sure to bring a lunch and something to drink," she added.

Sunshine handed him a folded sheet of paper with the riddle written on it. "Good luck!" she smiled, heading for the door. "I will call you later this afternoon. Would you like to meet me when you return from the library?"

"I'd like that very much," he answered.

After Sunshine left, Dakota read the riddle:

What is it?
It comes in different shapes and sizes.
Parts of it are curved, and some are straight.
You can put it anywhere,
but there is only one right place for it.

Dakota struggled with this riddle for almost an hour, but the moment he figured it out, a big grin spread across his face. He called room service and ordered a box lunch and coffee, and he asked the desk clerk to call for a taxi to take him to the library.

He approached the librarian and asked, "Where is the area of self-empowerment?"

She looked at him quietly for a moment, and then asked for the answer to the riddle.

He quickly replied, "A jigsaw puzzle piece."

The librarian smiled, handed him a key, and pointed to a door at the far end of the reading room. Dakota thanked her and headed toward the room. He unlocked the door and stepped inside. He heard a click as the door shut and locked behind him. He fumbled to find the light switch, and when the lights came on, he discovered there wasn't a handle on that side of the door. "Oh, no!" he exclaimed. "Now I'm stuck in here!"

He surveyed the room, only to find there weren't any windows, either. Shelves of books arranged in alphabetical order lined the walls. A desk and comfortable chair were the only furniture, and a box of matches on the desk seemed to be the only thing out of place. The most important feature seemed to be a large chest in the center of the room. "This is very interesting," Dakota observed. "It looks just like my personal treasure chest, but much larger."

Since Dakota's personal chest contained his learning nugget checklists, he suspected that this chest contained more valuable information for him. He approached the chest and saw a tag on the lock. It read:

At night they come without being summoned,
And by day they are lost without being taken.
Hint: They are always there.

Dakota thought about this puzzle for a while. Very pleased with himself, he answered out loud, "The stars! The answer is, the stars! Wow! What a clue!"

Dakota wondered what Uni might say to him. His imagination answered, "He'd probably say, 'A riddle is sometimes like real-life issues. The answer is usually not all that complicated, yet it is always a challenge until we see it in a different way.'

"This riddle is no different. The stars are like principles. Even though we can't always see them, they are always there."

Remembering Uni gave him a warm and secure feeling. He took a deep breath, swallowed, and set aside his emotions.

He moved to the row of books that had titles beginning with the letter S. There were several books about stars, but only one was titled *Stars of the night.* He took the book from the shelf, brushed off the dust, and opened it. What a surprise! The pages had been cut out to form a pocket. Inside the pocket was another key!

When Dakota used the key to open the chest, suddenly the walls began to close in on him. "What's happening here?" flashed across his mind, and his pulse began to race. "I need to figure this out quickly, or I'm going to be crushed," he gasped. Desperately he looked around, but couldn't find a clue. He tried to push the walls back, but no matter how hard he pushed, they steadily moved closer and closer. Panicking, Dakota tripped and fell against the chest. When he did, the lid slammed shut and the walls receded!

"Thank goodness," he sighed.

Shaken by the experience, he realized that the ⬩learning nuggets were still inside the chest. "Now what?" he wondered aloud.

He inspected the chest, and this time he noticed a compass embedded in the lid. An engraving below it read:

Look to the compass to find your true north.

"Interesting," Dakota murmured, remembering that Uni had explained the importance of our internal compass. "A navigator depends on the compass to determine true north," he had told Dakota.

"That's it!" Dakota realized. "I don't think I can pick up the chest, but I can turn it to face true north!"

The chest was heavy, but he managed to push it to face north. This time when he lifted the lid, the walls didn't move.

Inside the chest, he found a book titled, *Loser or Chooser?* Dakota lifted the book from the chest and seated himself in the comfortable chair next to the desk. He opened his Thermos, poured some coffee, and began to read.

Loser or Chooser?

Part One
Change Your Focus

There's no middle ground between loser and chooser. Choosers are action-driven people and each decision takes them forward. Losers make decisions that leave them in their comfort zone. They are either standing still or going downhill, because losers believe they don't have a choice.

In reality, the only thing we have 100% control over is our choices, and all choices come with consequences. The consequences can be either negative or positive. The key is to anticipate which they will be *before* we make a choice. Consider what happens when you pick up a stick. When you pick up one end the (choice), the other end comes with it (the consequence.) The direction of our lives and who we are is determined by the choices we make every day.

In life we can't control everything

Trying to control life is a losing battle. For example, we can't control the weather, unexpected situations, or how people think or act. Dwelling on things we cannot control wastes our energy and can lead to feelings of anxiety and anger.

What alternatives do we have over things we can't control?

Attitude is a choice. Be a chooser and change your focus.

Respond to things you can't control by acting like an oyster. The oyster has a big problem when a grain of sand gets into its shell and becomes a very important irritant. The oyster knows it can't rid itself of the grain of sand. At some point, the oyster accepted the truth and embraced the problem. From a painful, annoying situation eventually comes a beautiful pearl. Be a chooser! Change your attitude and watch as your life starts to change. As you gain inner strength, your self-confidence will increase.

Charles Swindoll in his book, *Strengthening Your Grip*, had this to say about attitude:[1]

This may shock you, but I believe the most significant decision I can make on a day-to-day basis is my choice of attitude. It is more important than my past, my education, my bankroll, my successes or failures, fame or pain, what other people think of me or say about me, my circumstances, or my position. Attitude is that "single string" that keeps me going or cripples my progress. It alone fuels my fire or assaults my hope. When my attitudes are right, there's no barrier too high, no valley too deep, no dream to extreme, no challenge too great for me.

Another reason for an attitude check is that most people don't enjoy being around those who have an "attitude deficiency disorder." It will just about eliminate your ability to have any influence with others.

We need a 10/90 attitude check

Charles Swindoll had it right when he said, 'Life is 10% what happens to you and 90% how you react to it.'

What does this mean? Imagine that someone said he would drive you to work and he arrived late. This threw your whole schedule off. That's 10% of what happened. The 90% is how you decide to react to the event. Do you have angry words with the driver about being late? Do you demand that he drives faster, only to end up with a traffic ticket and more lost time?

The driver blames you and has a yelling match with you about who is going to pay the ticket. Does the added stress determine how you treat people for the rest of the day? This only adds more unnecessary conflict. Do you feel that the event ruined your entire day? Why did you have a bad day? If you had stopped to adjust your attitude soon after the driver arrived late, the negative events would have ended then and there.

Becoming a person of influence is a choice.

We want to have the ability to influence the behaviors of others— we cannot force others to change or manipulate them.

We can influence others by modeling the behaviors we want others to follow.

We can have influence over a special cause by volunteering our time, energy, or resources.

We can influence others with encouragement and support and by demonstrating good character. We do this by living the action driven principles that shape our character.

Action-driven people shift their focus to become people of influence. Roger Staubach, the famous quarterback for the Dallas Cowboys, had a great influence on his team. His attitude was impossible not to lose and soon everybody on the team felt the same way.

The challenge of leadership is to be strong, but not rude: be kind, but not weak: be bold, but not bully: be thoughtful, but not lazy: be humble, but not timid: be proud, not arrogant: have humor, but without folly.
Jim Rohn

Dakota paused and thought about what he had just read. "I want to learn how to become a chooser and not a loser in life. Being a person of influence and shifting my attitude will help when I'm stuck with a problem I can't control."
Dakota turned the page and continued to read.

Part Two
The Land of Pause

The Land of Pause is a magical place. There, you are given a wireless remote that only you can control. There is only one button on this remote—it's the pause button.
The Land of Pause is where action-driven people take control over their choices and destiny. There they choose how to manage their life to deal with emotions.

We can't control our circumstances, but we can choose how to react.
The story of Dr. Viktor Frankl demonstrates the power of choice. Dr. Frankl was taken prisoner during the Holocaust. He survived unspeakable horrors in four Nazi concentration camps where his wife, his parents, and his only brother were killed. Dr. Frankl was definitely aware of things he could not control, yet he had the courage to focus his attitude and energy on what he could control. In his book, *Man's Search For Meaning*, he wrote: *Everything can be taken from a man but one thing: the last of the human freedoms—to choose one's attitude in any given set of circumstances, to choose one's own way.*

When Viktor Frankl wrote about the freedom to choose one's own way, he was referring to that space between situation (what's happening to us) and response (how we react.) This space is where we make choices. It is the Land of Pause.

Situation	The Land of Pause	Response
What's happening to us	Evaluate choices and consider the consequences	How we react to the situation

Viktor Frankl did not choose to be in a concentration camp. As children, we did not ask to be placed in foster care or to have a dysfunctional family, but we have the power to choose how we will react to those misfortunes. A quote by Viktor Frankl explains: '*When we no longer are able to change a situation, we are challenged to change ourselves.*'

Part Three
Nowhere Land

Nowhere Land is a place without a wireless remote. There, losers have learned to act only on their impulses and make decisions based on emotions. Instead of managing their emotions; they allow their emotions to manage them. When we are reactive, our emotions take over automatically, influencing how we think and how we behave and, therefore, how we conduct our lives.

How do you act when someone cuts you off in traffic? A reactive person may shout "Hey, you stupid jerk, watch where you're going." An action-driven person is grateful for avoiding an accident.

Do you know someone who loses control if you spill something? A reactive person may say, "How could you be so stupid? Watch what you're doing." An action-driven person will grab a towel"

Some people explode when they can't find their car keys. A reactive person will accuse someone else for taking them. An action-driven person will pause to think about where the keys might have been left, or will ask for help in finding them. These people tend to remain calm under stress.

Do you know someone who is constantly advising you how to do things? A reactive person may say, "Hey, get off my back and leave me alone." An action-driven person will thank the advisor for caring.

When people react based on their emotions, they often make poor decisions. Many times, those decisions are hurtful to others and to us. You might think of them as a hit-and-run collision. Hit-and-run people leave the damage behind.

Victim Behavior

People who live in Nowhere Land are the opposite of action-driven people. They engage in victim behavior and spend a huge amount of energy trying to control and change other people and circumstances.

They respond to life by blaming all their problems on their parents, teachers, or the foster care system. This allows them to avoid taking ownership for their lives, their actions, and who they are. It means that they have removed the only person who can bring about change in their lives.

When life presents you with the opportunity to make a choice, how will you choose to respond? Let's look at the difference between victim behaviors versus action-driven behaviors.

Victim Behaviors	Action Driven Behaviors
Make choices based on impulse.	Make choices based on key principles.
If life stirs you up, explode.	Maintain a calm, cool manner.
Blame others for their problems.	Take ownership of their problems.
Become a workaholic.	Balance work, family, and social activates.
Act aggressively or passively.	Act assertively.
Criticize others. Find fault.	Build the self-esteem of others.
Cave into peer pressure.	Charts their own path
Seek revenge.	Offer forgiveness.
Complain often.	Seek solutions.
Create power struggles.	Build understanding.
Use victim language.	Use positive language.
Float through life	Set goals.

One of our greatest opportunities for growth in life comes when we step out of our victim behaviors and move toward action-driven behaviors.

Dakota closed the book, realizing that he had read wise words that would change his life. "With this information, I will have more freedom and happiness than I've ever known before," he murmured. He put down the book, reached into his day pack, took out his journal, and began to write.

JOURNAL

When we pause, it gives us time to collect our thoughts and sort through our emotions before we act. This can be a difficult task at first, because it's not a natural habit. Yet it is one we can develop with practice. Remember the subconscious mind. The longer we practice going to The Land of Pause, the easier it will become. With practice, we will learn to go there naturally.

I can't control what happens to me, but I can use the pause button to make better choices. I no longer have to be a victim of my past circumstances. I have the freedom to choose my own way.

Dakota replaced his journal in his day pack and returned the book to the chest, locked it, and returned the key to its hidden place on the bookshelf. Now he had to solve the mystery of the room and find an exit.

"Let's see," he thought. "Maybe I can return the chest to the position it was in before I moved it to face true north." He leaned his full weight against one end of the treasure chest and pushed it back to its original position. "I was right!" he grinned as a small section of one wall silently slid backward. "At least the wall is moving in the right direction! This time it's not going to crush me to death!"

He crossed the room to the newly exposed section and looked down. Directly beneath his feet was a trap door! Lifting a flat handle on the surface of the door, he saw a ladder extending down into a pitch-black hole. A torch was mounted on the wall next to the ladder. Dakota chuckled, "So that's why there's a box of matches on the desk." He lit the torch.

"Well, here I go again—straight into another adventure!"

Balancing the lighted torch in one hand, he placed his foot on the top rung and climbed down into the darkness.

Cr-rack!

Dakota heard the wooden rung splinter before it broke beneath his weight. Dropping the torch, he grabbed the rung above with both hands and hung on for his life. The torch sputtered as it hit a shallow pool of water below. Before the flame was extinguished, Dakota looked down and saw hundreds of huge rats scurrying about, squealing their displeasure.

"Oh, no!" Dakota screamed. He feared rats even more than he hated snakes. "If one of those hideous rats bites me, I could get rat fever and gangrene—and I could die!" He shuddered and tightened his grip on the ladder rung.

Fumbling in the dark, he managed to regain his footing on a higher rung. Weak with terror, somehow he found the strength to pull himself back up the ladder to safety. He slammed the trap door shut. "I don't know whether rats can climb," he breathed, "but I'm certainly not taking any chances!"

Panting, he threw his body across the trap door and lay there waiting for his heart to resume an even beat. "What was I thinking!" he asked himself. "I know that a wrong choice can be deadly! Well, I've just learned a valuable lesson. I need to pause and think about the consequences before I make such an important decision."

Finally he rose from the floor and pondered his dilemma. "I still have to find a way out of here!" His eyes darted around the room, looking for a clue. Suddenly he realized he was facing true north. With revived energy, he began searching the north end of the room, and then the north end of the desk. Beneath the desktop, his fingers found a toggle switch! Excited, he snapped the switch from left to right.

Nothing happened.

"What next!" he moaned, shaking his head in disbelief.

But outside in the main reading room, the librarian heard a buzzing sound. She moved a matching toggle switch on the corner of her desk, and the door swung open.

"Now, that's better," Dakota said as he quickly left the room.

"Are you okay?" questioned the librarian. "You don't look so well."

"Yes! I'm fine," Dakota answered as he handed her the key to the room.

"I've been waiting for you to buzz me so I could leave." the librarian grumbled.

"Thank you," replied Dakota, practicing a newly learned action-driven response.

A taxi was waiting outside the library to take him back to his hotel. As he entered the lobby, the desk clerk greeted him. "I will page Miss Jones and let her know you have returned," he said.

In his room, Dakota collapsed on the bed. He was startled by the phone ringing. The room was almost dark. "I must have dozed off," he realized. He picked up the phone. "Hello," he answered, still half asleep.

"Hi," said Sunshine. "I'm calling to invite you to have a late dinner with me."

He was awake and alert immediately. "That sounds like a great idea!" he answered.

"Good! Then I'll meet you at the hotel restaurant in about an hour."

Dakota was excited at the thought of having dinner with Sunshine. Eager to make a good impression, he took extra time to shower and dress.

Arriving at the restaurant, he saw Sunshine at a table by a window. He almost didn't recognize her without her uniform. She was wearing a light blue dress, her hair fell softly around her shoulders, and she looked so beautiful. Dinner was delicious, and the conversation was even better.

Sunshine told him how much she enjoyed her role as guest coordinator. "Long ago, many people helped me to discover the wisdom that could be found here at Blue Mountain. This job is my way of giving back to them."

As he listened, Dakota realized he was discovering another principle, the principle of service—the idea that we need to give back what has been given to us by others. He thought he needed to explore this principle a little more, but that would have to wait. For now, he needed to concentrate on the matters at hand.

Sunshine asked, "What was the most difficult thing you learned today?"

"Well," Dakota answered, "I think because I have been more of a reactive person most of my life, having the discipline to pause will be a challenge for me—but one I can handle," he added confidently.

Sunshine replied, "That was a challenge for me, too. But with practice, all things are possible."

Dakota looked into Sunshine's eyes. "The best part of coming to Blue Mountain is meeting you. You give so much of yourself to help others. Not only are you beautiful, but you're beautiful on the inside. That's a special gift. I've already grown very fond of you and I think we've hit it off well. I'd like to get to know you better, if that's okay with you."

Sunshine blushed. "I would like that very much, Dakota. But it's important for you to finish your quest if we are to move forward with this relationship.

"I had to complete the same quest that you are following. I'm also from a dysfunctional family and I've moved around a lot. I struggled with my past and its effect on my life. We all need to learn how to be strong leaders and role models so we can help others who are struggling. When you have completed your quest, I hope you'll come back to Blue Mountain so we can spend time together and get to know each other better."

"You're right, Sunshine. I *will* come back—and when I do, we can finish our quest together."

"I'll look forward to that," Sunshine smiled.

After dinner, Dakota and Sunshine walked in the gardens that surrounded the restaurant. There was coolness in the air, and Dakota wrapped his jacket around Sunshine's shoulders. They found a comfortable bench away from the main area.

"Do you know where I go from here?" Dakota asked.

"Your next mission is to tour the battlefields in Nowhere Land," Sunshine answered.

"What!" he exclaimed. "You want me to go to Nowhere Land?"

"Yes, I do. I know that it will be difficult, but the journey will give you the opportunity to learn new life skills for dealing with conflict and building better relationships. You said earlier that you tended to be a reactive person, so it's really important for you to learn these skills."

"But I'm enjoying being in this peaceful place with you. Is it a good idea to tackle such a journey so soon?"

"I understand your apprehension, Dakota, but you won't be alone. A very good friend of mine, General Carlisle Parker, has agreed to go with you. General Parker has been like a grandfather to me. He is a strong role model who knows a lot about life and how to make the best of it. I'm sure he will be a great help to you. General Parker is retired from the Royal Australian Corps of Military Police. He can be rough-spoken at times, but he is also loyal and kind.

"Be careful in Nowhere Land," she warned. "The people who live there are content with who they are. They don't welcome change. They are not ready to be taught, but when they are, someone will be there to help them. We never give up hope, because everyone has the potential to grow."

Sunshine could see that Dakota was worried about his next mission. She let him express his feelings and listened to his concerns. As he adjusted his attitude to a more positive outlook, his enthusiasm returned, and Sunshine knew his next adventure would be a success.

"After you finish your mission with General Parker, I will be waiting for you. I'll clear all my appointments to spend time with you," she promised.

"I'd like that," Dakota nodded.

As they walked back to his hotel, they talked about how much they both wanted to help children and young adults who are dealing with some of the same issues they had dealt with. They recognized that being from dysfunctional families could be the bond for them to work on together in the future.

Back in his room, Dakota began to write in his journal—but it was less about what he had learned that day, and more about his growing affection and respect for Sunshine.

In the morning, Dakota packed all his belongs for his journey to the battlefields of Nowhere Land. He was glad that General Parker would be with him.

Over breakfast, Dakota reviewed his learning nugget checklist. He looked up to see a tall, strong, well-built older man dressed in military fatigues entering the restaurant. "This must be General Parker," Dakota thought. He stood up and gave a quick wave.

The General crossed the room to Dakota's table.

"Good morning! Are you Dakota Stone?" asked the General.

"Yes, and you must be General Parker."

"Are you ready to visit the battlefields, Dakota?"

"Yes, sir," he replied.

They loaded Dakota's luggage in the General's jeep and headed out of the city. At the gate, Dakota handed his checklist to the gatekeeper and waited for permission to continue.

The Learning Nuggets Checklist

• Self-empowerment is the process of taking control of our choices and understanding their consequences. The result is a decision about the way you choose to conduct yourself.
• Your choices are the only things in the universe that you have a 100% control over.
• All choices have consequences, either positive or negative.
• Attitude is a choice—it lets us be in control of our emotions.
• Life is 10% what happens to us, and 90% how we react to it.
• We can't control what happens to us, but we can use the pause button to make better choices. This gives us time to reframe our attitudes and behavior.
• Action-driven people base their decisions on values and principles, not impulse and emotions.
• Nowhere Land is a place without a wireless remote. There, people have learned to act only on their impulses and make decisions based on emotion.
• People in Nowhere Land engage in victim behaviors. They believe they don't have a choice.
• We want to have the skill to influence the behaviors of others—not to change, control, or manipulate them.
• People of influence are strong individuals with character.
• Become an action-driven person instead of a victim.

The gatekeeper nodded his approval "You have captured all the wisdom offered here," he said. "God bless, you may proceed."

CHAPTER SIX

THE BATTLEFIELDS

The drive to the battlefields was interrupted by what appeared to be a checkpoint. Standing in the middle of the road was a rugged man holding a rifle. The General brought the jeep to a halt.

"What's going on here, General?" Dakota asked

"Let me do all the talking," replied the General, "and we'll find out."

The gunman approached. "What's your business here?" he demanded.

"We're on our way to the battlefields. Is that a problem?" answered the General.

The gunman barked at Dakota. "What's your name?"

Dakota didn't want to show fear, so he looked the gunman in the eye and gave his name.

"Why in the world would anyone want to visit the battlefields?" questioned the gunman roughly.

The General's voice matched the gunman's. "We're here to study conflict resolution." Clearly, he was irritated. Dakota thought to himself, "I hope the General can resolve *this* conflict quickly."

"Let me see your passports," growled the gunman. The General handed him their documents.

"Now I'm going to give you a warning," said the gunman. "DO NOT bother any of the villagers while you're here. If you try to change anyone, you will be detained. IS THAT UNDERSTOOD?"

"NO PROBLEM!" snapped the General.

The gunman stepped back and waved them on. As they drove away, Dakota asked, "Does this happen often?"

"It's not unusual," replied the General. "You won't meet many people in Nowhere Land who are interested in being civil or changing their attitudes."

After driving in silence for a few minutes, the General said. "It's another two-hour drive to our hotel, so we have time to discuss a few details and talk about what we should look for at the battlefields."

"Fine," replied Dakota. "I was hoping you had some advice for me." He was starting to think of the General as a mentor.

"You see, son," he began. Dakota was surprised by the General calling him son. He thought, "I like the sound of that." He continued to listen to the General, but now with a sense of pride.

"It's a basic human need to have lasting, meaningful relationships, and almost everything we do in life involves relationships. We have relationships with our families, friends, co-workers, and with individuals within our communities. In fact, healthy relationships are an important ingredient to finding happiness. It's basically impossible to live life without interacting with others and it will be difficult to build quality relationships without knowing how to manage conflict. Pointing out a problem is easier than providing a solution or agreeing to be part of the solution.

"Conflict is a part of life. Since we all have different opinions, beliefs, and needs, we don't have to view disagreement as something negative or perceive it as a threat.

"Conflict is like using a hammer. We can use a hammer as a tool to build something, or we can use it as a tool to tear things down. Like a hammer, conflict can be a helpful device to improve relationships or a device that destroys relationships. The choice is yours."

Dakota thought to himself, "I can relate to the hammer. I have a way of damaging a good relationship before it can get started. I certainly don't want that to happen with Sunshine." He began to realize the importance of this part of the journey.

The General asked, "Have you given much thought to your motives when you're dealing with conflict?"

"No," Dakota admitted. "I'm afraid I haven't. What do motives have to do with it?"

The General explained. "We are responsible for our motives, just as we are responsible for our actions. Your motive for resolving conflict is not about deciding who is right or wrong, who said or did what, or who deserves the blame. It's not about being protective and defensive over your point of view. All of those motives create power struggles. A better motive occurs when you believe a solution is possible without resorting to insults, assigning blame, and imposing your views and beliefs on others.

Harriet Lerner wrote a book titled *The Dance of Anger*. In it, she wrote: *'We have a right to everything we think and feel — and so does everyone else. It is our job to state our thoughts and feelings clearly and to make responsible decisions that are congruent with our values and beliefs. It is not our job to make another person think and feel the way we do or the way we want them to.'*

"When you are faced with a power struggle, focus on what you can do. You can repeat the goal instead of responding to threats or name calling. It takes two to argue, and you can always refuse to participate. Avoiding power struggles can be difficult, but if it were easy, people would already be doing it.

"If your motive is about being controlling, the focus goes into winning."

"That can become an endless battle over words," Dakota remarked thoughtfully.

"Listening is another important step in resolving conflict," the General continued. "Let me explain. Effective listening requires us to put aside our thought for a moment and really listen to another person's point of view. Once you really understand that position, you can propose a solution that meets your needs while at the same time comes as close as possible to meeting the other person's needs

"Be courteous, and don't interrupt. Pay attention to your body language as well. Don't roll your eyes or shake your head. Body language is 90% of how we communicate, and what we say is only 10%."

The General continued, "Learn to use 'I' statements. They are effective because they state how you feel. 'You' statements are accusations that create defensiveness. It works like this:

"No one can deny how you feel. An 'I' statement simply says, 'When you do that, this is how I feel.' Once you have stated your feelings, listen for the response. If the person is defensive or laughs it off as a joke, remember that your motive is not to change the person's point of view, but to express your feelings. At that point, avoid getting pulled into a power struggle to prove your motives. Just calmly repeat your feeling.

"When someone expresses hurt feelings, you may not agree with that person. Empathy isn't about agreeing with someone, it's about understanding or recognizing the other person's feelings. It simply says you understand how that person feels. Denying someone's feelings will create frustration or increased anger."

Dakota asked, "Are there steps in resolving conflicts?"

The General laughed. "That's the hardest part." He reached into his jacket pocket and handed Dakota a folded sheet of paper listing five basic steps to resolving conflict.

"It would be easier for you to read this, since I'm driving," he said.

"That would be a smart thing to do," Dakota agreed. They laughed.

Conflict Resolution
Five basic steps to resolving conflict:

Step one—Use the principle of respect and accountability.
Start with the right mindset, 'honesty and trust.' Both agree to try to resolve the conflict.
Know your motives.
Use effective listening.
Use "I" statements.

Step two—Speaker states the problem clearly. Keep it short and to the point.
It's important to state only one issue at a time.
Speak calmly and rationally. Be aware of your body language.
The listener can restate the speaker's position. For example, "It sounds like you feel hurt because..."

Step three—Reverse roles and repeat step two.
The speaker now becomes the listener.

Step four—Explore alternative solutions.
Each party writes down possible solutions.
Discuss which ones come closest to meeting the needs of both parties.
If a solution cannot be reached, agree to disagree. (Without hostility)

Step five—Maintain integrity.
Follow through with the agreement.

Dakota finished reading the five steps. "General," he said, "many of us don't like to admit that we behave childishly when it comes to conflict. Too often we revert to anger, blame, and dishonesty. We become defensive and we try to rationalize our behavior. But I can see now that we don't have to remain that way. If we align action-driven principles with the five steps and follow the process, the answer will be automatic."

They drove quietly for a mile or two. Then the General said, "You seem to be deep in thought, Dakota."

"Yes, I was," Dakota answered. "Learning about the five steps is a lot to digest."

"The hotel is just around the bend. Let's get you settled in your room, and then we can relax and have dinner later."

Over dinner, the General explained the challenges ahead. His voice changed to a serious tone as he said, "Dakota, our visit to the battlefields tomorrow will be ugly and unpleasant. These battles are reenactments of conflicts between reactive people. Typically, they fail to pause and strategize about how they will manage the conflict. Without the ability to pause, they forge into battle with a full-scale assault. The other person, taken by surprise, becomes defensive, and then the battle escalates. Since conflict is a part of life, learning how to manage it is an important life skill. Unfortunately, reactive people are unaware that there are better ways to deal with disagreements."

"Thanks for the warning," said Dakota.

The General smiled, "Get some rest, son. I'll see you in the morning."

Day Two in Nowhere Land was chilly and overcast, with a hint of rain. As they started their trip, the General warned, "Don't get involved in the different conflicts, Dakota. These people are reenacting the conflict over and over again. They are inclined to turn on you just like they would do in real life. We are here to observe, not to get involved.

"Look at each conflict and see how action-driven principles could improve their relationships. Do you remember the three R's, the three C's, and good judgment?"

"Yes, I do," replied Dakota. "They are basic principles that define good character."

When they reached the first battle site, the General explained, "It was recorded that the battle that took place here was between a father and his son. The son wasn't taking responsibility for doing his homework, and he showed a lack of respect for his father."

The General parked the jeep at a distance, and the two men watched the battle.

In an angry voice, the boy shouted to his father, "I hate you! It's not fair for you to ground me! It's your fault, anyway. I asked you to help me with my homework, but you said you were too busy getting ready for your stupid trip."

Dakota heard much anger and criticism from both the father and his son. No one was winning this unpleasant confrontation. The homework didn't get done, and an important relationship was deteriorating.

Dakota shook his head. "The father had an opportunity to set an example by apologizing to his son and arranging for a tutor for the times he was out of town. The father then could ask the son for a commitment to get his homework done on time."

The General agreed with Dakota. "Apologizing is not an easy thing to do, but saying 'I'm sorry' can be a fast way to solve a small problem, and it can turn into an opportunity to strengthen a relationship. Trying to get even only prolongs the conflict.

"Even if you didn't do something on purpose, you still need to apologize. Be specific about the incident so the offended person knows exactly what you're apologizing for. It's very important to be sincere. People who admit they're wrong usually go farther in life than people who try to prove they're right."

The General went on to explain, "Successful families often have a decision-making process that helps them when problems occur. Through this process, their children learn to be respectful in the way they speak to their parents. These parents should include their children in opportunities to participate and share in decisions. When children take part in decision making, they feel they are important and have a chance to be heard. They also learn how to make decisions.

"Dr. Phil McGraw in his book, *Family First* wrote: '*The very frightening fact is that every time your children win a battle with you, they lose more of what they really want and need—trust in guidance.*'

The General and Dakota drove on to the next battle site. There, two friends were accusing each other of spreading rumors.

"How could you do this to me?" screamed Samantha. "I thought we were friends."

"You already told someone besides me, so I thought it was okay if I said something," Belinda screamed back.

"That's not true. You are lying. I'm never going to speak to you again," yelled Samantha

"Fine," Belinda snapped, "I never liked you anyway."

"Well, you're not going to get away with this. I'll get even," Samantha snapped back.

They both stormed off.

Dakota turned to the General. "Broken promises can cause distrust and can damage one's character."

The General nodded his approval. "You have learned this lesson well," he told Dakota. "It also appears they broke every one of the five steps plus the action-driven principles. Parents need to take a role in teaching their children how to interact with each other."

When they reached the next battle site, they saw two young men, Jorge and Jim, who were arguing. Jorge shouted, "You promised to pay back the money you borrowed. I need that money to pay for my books. You never care about anyone but yourself. You're a jerk, and I can't trust you. Don't ever ask me for anything again."

"Fine," Jim shouted back. He floored the gas pedal and left Jorge at the curb.

Jorge swore and shook his fist as Jim drove off.

"Did either young man win this argument?" asked the General.

"No," Dakota answered quietly. "Jim didn't keep his promise, and they both lost a good friend."

The General said, "This is a good time to explain the importance of being assertive and avoid naming calling. When hurts are not handled properly, they will surface later with either aggressive, blow-up anger or passive, clam-up behavior. We need to learn to speak the truth in love.

"With aggressiveness, people speak the truth but use harsh words. Anger can easily turn into hostility. Hostility can be expressed by screaming, hitting, slamming doors, slamming pots and pans, or driving aggressively. I'm hurting and I want you to hurt, too, is what the injured person is expressing. Getting even is another way of expressing this pain. Using the silent treatment also sends the same message.

"Passive behavior shows a lack of respect for one's own values, needs, or rights and they avoid conflict at any cost. This anger is often expressed in kind words that hide the truth. Although done in the interest of love, not rocking the boat, or maintaining peace at any price, feelings stay bottled up inside, ready to erupt at the drop of a hat."

"Build up anger is like a house without a chimney," Dakota commented. "If you don't have a chimney to ventilate the house, you won't be able to live in it."

"Exactly," the General agreed. "Passive anger has a long memory. It tends to hold a grudge. Assertiveness is the alternative to both passive and aggressive anger."

Dakota smiled. "I get it! Conflicts are inevitable, but anger, hostility, and resentment don't have to be."

They drove quietly for several miles. As they approached the next site, they could hear two parents arguing about how to deal with their daughter who hadn't done her chores. Both parents were doing their share of name calling and shouting. One blamed the other for being too easy, while the other blamed that parent for being too strict. The child was pleased, at least for the moment, because she was no longer the main subject. She just walked away and turned on the TV. The disagreement was still going on as Dakota and the General drove off.

Dakota said, "I feel sorry for their daughter. Parents need to learn how to find common ground without arguing in front of their children. In fact, she pretended not to care, but she hated it when her parents argued."

The General agreed. "Although parents have the leader's role, children's personal views and efforts should be encouraged. Having rules and knowing each other's role gives direction and structure to daily life. Routines and rules define and help family members know whose job it is to do what, when, in what order, and how often."

At the next battle site, a young man was attempting to return an iPod that wasn't working. Unfortunately, the warranty had expired. Manuel was angry, but the clerk listened to him calmly. Manuel began to raise his voice angrily. In this battle, Manuel allowed his emotions to control him, and he was escorted out of the store by Security.

The General explained, "Manuel was wrong because the warranty had expired. Sometimes we just need to admit when we are at fault and accept the consequences."

As the General and Dakota reached the next battlefield, they saw two girls arguing about voting for prom queen. Both girls were pushing their views on the other, and the argument was getting nasty. Dakota could see that there would be no winners in this battle. It was simply a difference of opinion, but the girls couldn't agree to disagree. Without that option, they allowed differing opinions to tear down their friendship.

As they drove through the battlefields, Dakota and the General observed many different battles—people cutting in line, arguments over traffic accidents, and siblings fighting. All allowed their emotions and frustrations to escalate into blame, anger, hostility, shouting, and name calling. No one apologized or took ownership of their actions. No one tried to take a time out. Some arguments ended in physical violence. There was a total lack of respect for anyone else's opinions or feelings. No one was trying to understand how the other person felt.

Dakota summed up their observations. "So many different conflicts, but the results were always the same—no winners, only losers. I get the point, General. I have seen enough reactive behaviors for one day."

"Knowing how to deal with conflict has many benefits," the General concluded. "Every time we resolve conflict with someone in a positive way, it strengthens that relationship. Once we understand that, we can begin to look at conflict as an opportunity instead of an obstacle.

"Over time, mismanaging conflict can also create health issues," the General added, "everything from headaches, high blood pressure, anxiety, depression, and other symptoms. That gives us another reason to learn how to manage conflict."

As they drove back to their hotel, Dakota said, "General, you were right. This was a very unpleasant tour. I need to clear my mind and get rid of all these negative feelings."

The General nodded, "I understand. Take this evening off, and we'll meet in the morning to continue your mission."

With that, the General left Dakota to his own thoughts.

Dakota sadly thought about the tour. He could even relate to some of the conflicts.

"I need to have a different mindset about conflict," he decided. "Resolving conflict depends upon having the mindset to solve the problem, not to win the argument. There are many options available to resolve conflict, and I must seek them out. I will never again approach conflict as a battle, but as an opportunity for two people to work together unselfishly to solve a problem. These are important learning nuggets to help my wounded child move forward out of the past."

As they arrived at the hotel, the General said, "Goodnight son. Call me in the morning when you are ready to meet."

Dakota entered his room and was eager to unwind after the long, cold day. As he sat at his desk, he thought about young adults who face conflict every day, often without the knowledge to manage peer pressure, disagreements, teasing, criticism, jealousy, and violent behavior. They tend to be reactive and ready to do battle without thinking. It is a challenge for them to manage conflict with a new mindset. He thought about the parents who were like children themselves when it came to dealing with conflict.

"We need to have more understanding before we judge others and their actions," he realized. "Often we assume we know what the other person's motives are, and we think we have a right to judge that person. What we believe depends on the clarity of our viewpoint."

Dakota remembered a story he had read by an unknown author.

A young couple moved into a new neighborhood. While they were eating breakfast on the first morning, the young woman saw her neighbor hanging laundry outside. "That laundry is not very clean," she said. "That woman doesn't know how to wash properly. Perhaps she needs better laundry soap." Her husband looked on, but remained silent.

Every time the neighbor hung her laundry to dry, the young woman made the same comments.

Several weeks later, the woman was surprised to see clean laundry hanging on her neighbor's line. She said to her husband, "Look! She has learned how to wash! I wonder who taught her to do that."

The husband said, "I got up early this morning and washed our windows."

How true this is in real life. We often judge others based on our own perceptions and views. What if the woman had met the neighbor and mentioned her dirty laundry? I'm sure the neighbor would have disagreed with that point of view. What we believe to be true is only a piece of the whole picture. Without having a complete picture, we have incomplete information.

Dakota opened his journal and began to write.

JOURNAL

My thoughts about conflict

It's not the conflict that damages a relationship, but it's how we process it that makes a difference. The process can be difficult, but there are tools we can use to resolve the conflict. During these times, we are tempted to give up or give in. Resist that path! Stay in the process! When I am focused on the results, I'm not in the process. When I stay in the process, the results will be automatic.

No matter how badly someone acts, I'm responsible for my behavior. I choose to behave in a certain manner because that's the type of person I am or want to become, not because someone will change or respond differently.

Dakota realized that he had not handled conflict well in the past. He usually avoided it until he was so upset that he said things to hurt the other person. He was grateful for the valuable nuggets he had learned that day.

"Before I call Sunshine," he thought, "I need to work on my nuggets list. Heaven only knows what will happen tomorrow!"

Dakota eagerly took out a sheet of paper and began to write.

The Learning Nuggets Checklist

Conflict Resolution

• Conflict is a natural part of life. We can use it to build relationships or tear them down.

• Use the five basic steps for resolving conflict.

• Stay in the process, and the results will be automatic.

• Apologize early and often.

• Know your motives to prevent power struggles.

• Be assertive. Address problems quickly to avoid blow-up or clam-up anger.

• Be careful not to judge others. What we believe depends on the clarity of our view—the window we are looking through.

When Dakota finished the list, he placed it in the room safe along with his journal, instruction manual, and his personal treasure chest.

"Now is a good time to call Sunshine," he decided. "I have so much to talk about with her tonight."

Dakota's phone call lasted well past midnight. Finally, and reluctantly, he said, "It's getting late, Sunshine, I'll call you tomorrow."

He hung up the phone and smiled. "To be continued," he murmured. Then he added, "I hope!"

He turned off the lights and fell into a deep sleep.

CHAPTER SEVEN

THE LOST MEDALLION

Dakota was awakened abruptly by heavy pounding on his door. "Dakota! Dakota! Wake up! It's the General."

As Dakota opened the door, the General pushed by.

"Get dressed quickly! No questions," he ordered.

Baffled by the urgency in the General's voice, Dakota didn't hesitate to obey the command. He threw on jeans, shirt, and a jacket while the General stuffed his passport, wallet, and toiletries into a small duffel bag.

"Let's go!" the General snapped as he hurried Dakota out the door.

Outside, an armed man in the General's jeep shouted, "Get in! Let's get out of here!"

As they drove away, a perplexed Dakota asked, "What's going on and where are we going?"

The General leaned back in his seat and took a deep breath.

"Your journey of self-discovery is almost finished, Dakota. In the final step of your quest, your mission is to find the cup of wisdom and drink its contents. Unless you do this, all the learning nuggets you have gathered and recorded on your checklists will be erased, and all you have learned will be forgotten."

"Wow!" Dakota exclaimed, "I certainly don't want that to happen! Where will I find the cup, General?

"The cup is hidden deep inside the Cave of Swimmers in the Libyan Desert of southwestern Egypt. We are on our way to the airport to catch a jet to Egypt. But we are in grave danger, Dakota. I've suspected that we were being followed, and now I know for sure that it's true."

"Akua had the same suspicions! Are these the same people Akua warned me about on the boat?"

"Yes, they will do anything to find the cup of wisdom before you do. They believe the cup will give them the wisdom and power to control others and prevent them from learning the truth about their past. They don't understand that wisdom is not about power and control. Instead, wisdom teaches us how to use knowledge. Without wisdom, we lack the ability to choose between right and wrong."

"If the cup is hidden inside the cave," Dakota asked, "how will I find it?"

"Its hiding place is marked with an ancient symbol embedded in the wall of the cave. When a matching symbol is placed inside it, together they become a key to unlock the cup of wisdom.

"In the entire world, there are only two medallions that match the same symbol in the cave. Earlier tonight, a courier was on his way to deliver one of the medallions to me at our hotel. On the way, the courier was ambushed and the medallion was stolen by the same men who are following us now.

"The only other matching medallion is in the hands of Professor Abu of Tanta University, sixty miles from Cairo. We must get the matching medallion from the Professor, and we must get to the cave before the militants."

The General reached into an inside pocket of his jacket and brought out a drawing of the medallion. Dakota studied the drawing with curiosity. Finally he said, "That's awesome, General!"

"That it is," replied the General.

Dakota was beginning to understand the danger he was in.

"Thank you for saving my life," he said gratefully.

"You're welcome," the General answered. "Sunshine would have my head if I let anything happen to you."

They both smiled.

At the airport, they drove out across the tarmac and boarded a private jet.

"This will be a long trip," the General said as they fastened their seatbelts. "Strange as it may seem, although today is early Tuesday morning in Australia, it's still Monday in Egypt."

"That should mess up our body clocks for a while," Dakota laughed.

"The trip will take at least 22 hours," the General continued. "We'll stop in Bangkok to refuel, but we won't have to get off the plane. I don't know exactly what will happen when we land in Egypt, but there will be people waiting to help us."

Once onboard, an attendant offered sandwiches, fruit, and coffee. Dakota picked at his food. He was too exhausted to eat. Every bit of energy was drained from his body. He hadn't gone to bed until after midnight and his sleep had been interrupted shortly after.

The General saw his eyelids closing and gently said, "The seats on this plane are built to fold flat to make a bed. Let's get some rest." He folded down his seat and Dakota did the same.

Soon they were sound asleep.

Many hours later, the pilot alerted them that they were two hours from the Egyptian border.

"We need to shower and have something to eat before we land," the General told Dakota.

The hot shower and meal revived their strength and spirits after the long journey. Just as they finished eating, the pilot's voice came over the speaker system. "Buckle up! We're about to land."

He brought the plane down at a private airport in Cairo, where a jeep was waiting to take them to the Nile River.

"Wow! How did you plan all of this at the last minute?" questioned Dakota.

"It's not important," the General answered. "Just be glad we are safe for now."

When they reached the Nile, they boarded a small sailing barge to take them downriver to Tanta.

"Welcome aboard," the captain greeted them. "The river current is strong enough to take us to Tanta without raising the sail." And so it did, with the help of four oarsmen, two on each side of the barge to navigate the waters.

"The scenery along the Nile is stunning," said the captain, "so sit back and enjoy the trip." He gave a command to the oarsmen, and they pushed away from the dock. A few minutes later, the captain joined his guests.

"Well, Dakota, this is your first visit to Egypt—and already you're traveling the Nile, the longest river in the world. It flows for more than 4,000 miles—but we're turning onto a branch that will take us north to Tanta, only 60 miles or so."

The barge moved briskly away from the city. Following the captain's invitation, Dakota soon was captivated by fascinating glimpses of life along the river. In the rich delta soil, fields of cotton and wheat flourished and nut trees grew in abundance. Along the shore, water buffalos were calmly chewing river plants, unaware of any barge activity on the water. The barge passed through villages with small houses made of mud bricks, some with shelter for the family livestock built atop the roofs. Children tending their sheep and goats waved to the travelers as the barge passed by.

"What friendly people!" Dakota exclaimed.

The captain answered, "Yes, they are. The people here in rural Egypt live very much the same way as their ancestors lived in biblical times."

Dakota closed his eyes and listened to the waves slapping steadily against the barge. From far off, a donkey's plaintive bray pierced the air. Passing a village, he heard a gentle call to prayer from a nearby mosque. "This is the most relaxing thing I've ever done," he murmured contentedly.

He was jolted back to reality when the captain touched his shoulder. "We'll be docking in a few minutes," he announced. "A car is waiting to take you to your destination."

Again, Dakota was amazed at how thoroughly the General had arranged every detail of their journey.

They gathered their few belongings and thanked the captain and crew as they exited the barge. Their driver was waiting patiently at the dock. He drove the car skillfully in and out of the dense and noisy city traffic, and they arrived at the university just as the sun was setting.

Entering the university campus, the General addressed a security guard at the gate. "Excuse me, sir. I'm looking for Professor Abu"

"I'll call him and let him know you are here. What is your name?"

"Tell him General Parker wishes to speak with him."

After a short conversation, the guard said, "Professor Abu asks that you wait here."

In just a few minutes, they saw a well-dressed small-boned man, not above five-and-a-half feet in height, crossing the lawn and approaching the gate. "Are you General Parker?" he asked.

"Yes, I am."

Professor Abu extended his hand in greeting. "You're fortunate that the university is open late tonight," he smiled, but he looked about nervously before speaking again. "I got a call that you would be arriving. Please follow me to my office."

When the three men were inside the office, Professor Abu locked the door and drew the shades. "No point in taking chances," he said. "Certain tribesmen in the area are dangerous. Recently they seized a group of tourists and demanded a large ransom before killing them all."

Without speaking, the General brought out the drawing of the medallion and handed it to Professor Abu. The Professor was quiet for a moment. Then he crossed the room, moved a framed painting behind his desk, and revealed a small wall safe. He adjusted the dial, and the safe swung open. With great care, Professor Abu took out a velvet pouch and handed it to the General. Inside was the ancient medallion!

"Magnificent!" the General breathed. He slipped the golden medallion back into its velvet pouch and carefully zipped it into an inside pocket in his jacket.

The professor locked the safe and moved the painting back in place. He was about to speak when the phone rang. As he listened to the caller, his eyes widened. Without a word, he reached under his desk and pressed a switch. Behind him, a bookcase pivoted on silent hinges, exposing a closed door.

"Leave quickly," he said. "Armed men are on their way here. Go to the roof. You will be met by friends who will take you to the Cave of Swimmers. Be careful! Now go, before the men reach this office!"

Dakota opened the door and found a flight of stairs leading upward. The General reached into his military pack and brought out a flashlight. They began to climb the stairs.

"Quiet!" warned the General. "Someone is standing at the top of the stairs!"

They froze with fear as two men dressed in military fatigues started down the stairs toward them. One of the men whispered loudly, "Come up here! Be quick! We know who you are."

"Is this a trap?" flashed across Dakota's mind.

The two strangers turned to ascend the stairs, with Dakota and the General following. "What choice do we have?" Dakota thought. "The door to Professor Abu's office locked behind us when we started up the stairs."

When they reached the roof, they saw that a helicopter had landed there. One of the uniformed men spoke. "My name is Jack, and this is my pilot, Ben. We are members of a special military team sent here to take you to the Cave of Swimmers."

Dakota sighed with relief. The strangers could be trusted!

The pilot boarded the helicopter first, and the other three were right behind him.

"Is everyone buckled in?" Ben shouted over the roar of the engine.

"We're ready for takeoff," Jack shouted back.

"Let's get out of here," Dakota called to Ben. "It's getting so I don't like surprises."

When they were safely in the air, fatigue and jet lag finally caught up with Dakota and General Parker. "This is going to be a long night," the General said wryly.

The helicopter didn't offer the comfort of the airplane. The noise level prevented anything but the shortest conversations, and the seats were barely padded. Despite the chaos, the General and Dakota drifted in and out of sleep.

Hours later, they heard Jack's voice waking them. "Okay, guys, we're here."

Dakota looked out the window. They had left the city far behind, and now they had landed on a rocky plateau deep in the mountains.

"Where are we?" Dakota asked sleepily.

"We've arrived at the Cave of Swimmers," Jack answered.

Dakota turned to the General. "Then my quest is almost finished," he said.

The General nodded his head, "Almost, son."

Dakota, the General, and Jack hopped out of the helicopter. When they were safely away from the whirling blades, Ben lifted the chopper and took off. Jack assured them that Ben would come back to get them. "That's if we are still alive," he added. A cold shiver ran down Dakota's back, but then he heard Jack calling to him. "Come on, Dakota! I know a shortcut inside."

The opening to the shortcut was only large enough for one person to squeeze through at a time. Once all three men were inside, the General turned on his flashlight. In the dim light, he showed the medallion to Dakota and Jack. Immediately they began to examine the cave walls in search of a matching symbol.

"Will you look at this!" said the General. "There are ancient paintings on the wall that look like people swimming. That's strange to see in the middle of the desert."

Jack replied, "Maybe this area wasn't always a desert."

"Good point," said the General.

"That's interesting," Dakota remarked. "I thought those marks at the bottom of the medallion were just scratches, but I think they're the same as the paintings on the wall."

The General compared the paintings of the swimmers to the medallion. "So they are," he agreed. "We must be getting close to the hidden cup."

He replaced the medallion in his inside pocket and continued down the passageway, with Jack and Dakota a few steps behind him. They were fascinated by the paintings, barely noticing anything else around them.

Dakota felt a sudden rush of terror. "General!" he screamed, "I'm falling!"

The General and Jack whirled around in time to see Dakota's shoulders and head disappearing into a hole in the floor. It had collapsed under his weight!

Stunned by the fall, Dakota lay at the bottom of a shallow pit, where he had landed on a mound of soft sand. Looking up, he saw the General and Jack on hands and knees, peering over the edge of the hole. "Are you all right?" the General called down.

Dakota felt his legs and arms. Nothing seemed to be broken. "I think so," he called to the men, "but I think I'd better rest here for a minute or two 'til I get my bearings."

Looking about him, he saw that he was not in a pit—he had fallen into a large room carved from a lower level of the cave. He was relieved to see that it was not more than seven feet deep and he'd be able to climb out with help from his friends above.

As Dakota gradually sat up, he became aware that the room was bathed in a strange, almost magical glow. Carefully he stood up and dusted off the sand. The glow was coming from an object at the far end of the room. His eyes opened wide as he realized what he was seeing.

Above him, General Parker and Jack heard Dakota's excited cries.

"Oh, my gosh! I see it, I see it! I've found the cup of wisdom! It's right here at the end of this room!"

The General couldn't believe what he was hearing. The words were caught in his throat for a second. "Holy smoke!" he shouted. "Are you sure it's the cup?"

"Yes!" Yes! There are stepping stone leading to it! General, toss me the medallion."

The General moved toward the edge of the opening. As he did, a few large rocks gave way. Dakota caught the medallion at the same time that a large rock landed on one of the stepping stones. When it landed, the floor opened. Below was a pit filled with writhing scorpions.

"I could be at the bottom of that pit if it weren't for that rock falling!" Dakota realized.

Jack was peering over the General's shoulder. "Be careful!" he called down to Dakota. "There may be more traps protecting the cup."

Dakota picked up a rock and tossed it onto another stepping stone. Nothing happened. He carefully stepped on that stone and threw another rock ahead of him. Again, nothing happened. "That's good!" he murmured. He continued to toss a heavy rock on each stepping stone until he had safely navigated his way to the cup.

With trembling hands, he grasped the cup, but it wouldn't budge from its place on the pedestal. Then he remembered the medallion. But where was the matching symbol? He searched the side of the pedestal. Nothing! But then he saw a flash of gold gleaming from the cave wall. There it was! He placed the gold medallion into the symbol and carefully turned it until it was locked in place. He closed his eyes as he reached for the cup—and the cup was released!

He could barely believe that he was holding the cup—a goblet of shining gold. Around the base was a circle of colorful gems. An inscription around the rim read, "Follow the path of true wisdom." Inside the cup was a small vial holding a clear, colorless liquid. Dakota carefully placed the vial and the cup in his day pack and headed back through the stepping stones, being certain to bypass the scorpion pit.

"What's happening, Dakota? Do you have the cup?" the General called down.

"Yes, I do," replied Dakota. "Help me get out of here!"

Jack reached into his military pack, brought out a sturdy rope, and tossed it down to Dakota. "Wrap the rope around your waist and we'll pull you up," he called.

Soon Dakota was safely above with the General and Jack. Beaming with pride, he took the cup and vial from his day pack and handed them to the General.

"You did it, son!" he praised.

The General and Jack studied the cup for a few minutes. "Just look at this magnificent cup!" said the General with awe. Jack patted Dakota on the back as the General placed the cup and vial in his military pack.

Jack pointed to a passageway and they headed toward the shortcut that would take them out of the cave.

They had gone a short distance when Dakota halted abruptly. "Listen!" he whispered. "I think I hear something."

The General turned off his flashlight, and they hid behind a huge boulder.

Four armed soldiers shinning their flashlights emerged from the darkness. As the light flashed by their hiding place, Dakota's heart began to beat faster. He was sure the gunmen could hear it. The soldiers were talking loudly, but in a language neither he nor the General understood. Finding nothing, the gunmen returned to the passage from where they had emerged. Their voices faded in the distance.

"Whew! That was close," Dakota breathed aloud. "I wonder what they were saying."

"I understood their language," Jack told them. "They're looking for the cup of wisdom."

Jack called Ben on a hand radio. "Hurry!' he ordered. "We need to get out of here *now*! We'll meet you at the drop-off."

The three men turned and headed down another passage that would take them back to the cave opening. Just as they reached the last turn to the opening, they saw flickering lights behind them.

"It's the soldiers!" Jack gasped. "Run! Run!"

They raced toward the cave opening. Jack and the General squeezed through just as Ben flew over the horizon. The men ran to the hovering helicopter and scrambled aboard.

"Where's Dakota?" Ben shouted over the noise of the blades.

"I don't know," Jack shouted back. "I thought he was right behind me."

But Dakota was still inside the cave! He had tripped and fell over a rock and twisted his ankle. From the passageway behind him, he heard heavy footsteps running toward him. "I've got to get out of here." His instincts told him.

Forgetting about his ankle, he picked himself up. With one great burst of energy he wriggled through the opening. Outside at last, he hurried toward the helicopter.

In what seemed to be only an instant later, one of the soldiers squeezed through the opening. The soldier raised his rifle, aimed, and fired. Bullets whizzed past Dakota's head and grazed the side of the helicopter.

"We can't wait any longer!" Ben shouted. He pointed to a rope ladder attached to the floor by the door. "Throw that to Dakota," he ordered as he lifted the helicopter into the air.

Jack tossed the rope ladder out the helicopter door. "Here, Dakota!" he yelled. "Catch!"

Dakota leaped into the air and grabbed the end of the rope ladder, hanging on with every bit of strength he could muster. Behind him, the soldier fired again. "Go! Go!" Dakota screamed. "Go!"

Ben pulled up and away, and Dakota sailed through the air beneath the retreating helicopter.

When they had cleared the gunfire, Ben slowed down so Jack and the General could pull Dakota into the helicopter to safety.

"That was *too* close!" Dakota sighed. "What a ride!" He closed his eyes and said a heartfelt prayer of thanks.

All four agreed they were glad the ordeal at the Cave of Swimmers was behind them.

Ben handed Jack a Thermos of coffee, and Jack poured four cups. Raising his cup in a toast, the General laughed with relief.

"To Cairo! Here we come!"

Ten minutes before landing back in Cairo, Jack told Dakota and the General, "There will be a private jet waiting, to take you and the treasure safely to Australia."

The General thanked Jack and Ben for all their help. "You're welcome," Jack replied. "We're always here if you need us. We have served our country, and we are glad this mission ended so successfully."

Dakota watched and listened as the men interacted. "What respect they have for one another," he thought. "That's the kind of mutual respect I want in my life. That's the kind of care and concern that families give to each other. They are there whenever another family member needs them." A wave of sadness passed over him. "I wish I had a family like that," he let himself think. Then he dismissed his thoughts and thanked Jack and Ben for helping him to finish his quest.

They landed in Cairo and made a smooth exchange from helicopter to airplane. Once the plane was in the air, the General and Dakota unbuckled their seatbelts. "Let's get cleaned up," the General said.

They showered and dressed in clean clothes from the supply on board. An attendant brought them a welcomed hot meal. They hadn't eaten since before arriving in Egypt. "Was that really just yesterday," Dakota thought in amazement.

While they ate, Dakota suddenly remembered, "We left Australia so fast, I left behind my treasure chest, journal, instruction manual, and checklists. I locked them in the safe in my room. What if they fall into the wrong hands?"

"It's okay," the General answered. "I left orders to send your things to my ranch outside of Blackheath. The ranch is a perfect place to escape—and we've certainly earned some rest and relaxation!

"You'll like my ranch," he continued. "There are amazing views of Blue Mountain from my front porch. Do you like horseback riding?"

"Love it," Dakota replied.

"Well, that's high on the list at our next destination," he promised.

The long flight back to Australia was uneventful—and that was just fine with Dakota.

The plane landed at a private airport in Sydney, where the General's jeep was parked and ready for the drive to Blue Mountain. The area and the ranch were all the General had promised.

"Wow! Dakota cried. "This is absolutely beautiful! It's so peaceful and quiet! Sure beats what we've been through lately."

Inside the cabin, all their belongings from Nowhere Land were stacked in the middle of the livingroom.

"After we settle in, we can go for a walk along the creek and enjoy a bit of nature," the General said. "When we come back, I'll fire up the barbe."

The refrigerator and pantries were well stocked. "You have a way of planning for everything," Dakota said in admiration. "I guess that's why you're a General."

The ringing of the phone interrupted their conversation. "Hello, Jack," said the General. "Yes, the flight was smooth and we're both fine." He listened to Jack's voice for a few minutes. Then he said. "Thank you for that good information."

He hung up the phone and turned to Dakota. "Great news! The soldiers were caught and now they're where they belong—in jail."

They gave each other a happy high-five.

"I'll give Sunshine a call and let her know that we're back safely," said Dakota. "This will be a quick call so we can have that peaceful walk."

The General nodded his head and smiled.

CHAPTER EIGHT

ROCKS, DEPOSITS, BOUNDARIES

Dakota was awakened by sunlight shining into his room. He felt content and happy, knowing he and the General were safe and back in Australia. The thought of seeing Sunshine soon flashed through his mind.

"Hey! Dakota! Breakfast is ready," the General called from the kitchen.

"Be right there," Dakota called back.

After a hearty breakfast, the two men saddled horses and rode through the beautiful mountain trails. Three hours later, they returned to the cabin, removed the saddles, rubbed down the horses, and put them in a fenced pasture.

"What a perfect way to experience nature at her best," said Dakota. "I could get in a habit of doing this!"

"It's the best way to put life on hold and unwind," the General answered. "Come on! I'll fix some lunch."

The General loved to cook and Dakota enjoyed all the pampering, but he did help with the dishes. When the kitchen was clean, the General turned to him.

"Okay, son" he said. "Now that the work is done, it's time to enjoy this gorgeous day. Let's sit out on the porch."

Settling into a comfortable chair, Dakota cleared his throat, "General," he began, "I have a problem that I'd like to talk about, and I'd like your advice."

"Sure, Dakota. What's on your mind?"

Dakota stretched a loose thread on his jeans, avoiding the General's eyes. Finally he said, "I have a problem with relationships. I think people should know how I feel, and I don't think I need to express my feelings all the time. People think I'm stand-offish and cold, and they leave me.

"I'm growing fond of Sunshine, and we get along well together. I'm afraid at some point I'll mess up and she will leave me. I don't want that to happen!"

"I understand," replied the General. "I think the learning nuggets you are about to hear will help you establish better relationships from now on."

He asked Dakota, "What would happen to a car if you failed to change the oil, take care of the tires, or change the wiper blades?"

"The car would start to break down," Dakota replied.

"What would happen to indoor plants if you didn't water or fertilize them? What would happen if they didn't have the right amount of sunlight?"

"I don't think they would last long," Dakota answered.

"That's right. They would wither and die. Relationships are no different. If we fail to maintain our relationships, they will start to break down or wither and die.

"Every person has a basic need to be loved, valued, respected, appreciated, and understood. We must acknowledge those needs if we want to grow and maintain healthy relationships.

"An unknown professor, who wanted to drive home a point to his students, used a simple model to explain the lesson, and I will illustrate that lesson to you."

The General set up a small folding table, a large jar, some rocks about 2 inches in diameter, a box of pebbles, and a box of sand. He picked up the empty jar and proceeded to fill it to the brim with rocks.

"Is the jar full?" he asked Dakota.

Dakota nodded his head. "I can agree with that. The jar is full."

So the General picked up the box of pebbles and poured them into the jar. He shook the jar lightly, and the pebbles rolled into the open areas around the rocks. He asked Dakota "Is the jar full now?"

Again Dakota answered, "Yes now it's full."

He laughed as the General picked up the box of sand and poured it into the jar. The sand quickly filled up every space around the rocks and pebbles.

"Now," the General continued, "Dakota, I want you to recognize that this jar represents your life. The big rocks are the important things— your family, loved ones, your health and personal growth. If everything else were gone and only the big rocks remained, your life would still be full. The pebbles are the other things that matter—your work, your house, your car. The sand is everything else—the small stuff. The little stuff will have a way to overwhelm you and leave you with little time for the big stuff."

"When you put the sand into the jar first, there will be no room for the pebbles or the rocks. Put your energy into things that are vital to your happiness. Spend time with your family and play with your children. Take care of yourself and get medical checkups. Take time for community and your faith. What are the big rocks in your life Dakota?"

"I totally get that," said an enthusiastic Dakota "I'll take care of the big rocks first—the things that really matter. If I don't put the big rocks in first, I'll never get them in at all!"

The General smiled his approval. Then he disappeared into the kitchen. When he returned to the porch, he was carrying two cookie jars. One was empty, and the other jar was full of cookies. Dakota wondered what his friend was up to now. The General smiled as if he knew what Dakota was thinking.

"Imagine that every relationship starts with an empty jar. We build strong relationships by making deposits in the jar. Assume that a cookie is deposited each time one person in the relationship does a small act of kindness, provides words of encouragement, takes time to be a good listener, shows appreciation, or gives recognition.

Each deposit made into the cookie jar is will reinforce the idea that the relationship is important.

"When either person does the complete opposite, a withdrawal is made. A withdrawal occurs when either one is selfish, disrespectful, doesn't keep a commitment, or finds fault unnecessarily. That person is removing from the jar rather than adding to it. Each withdrawal emphasizes the idea that the person doesn't care about the relationship.

"If there are more withdrawals then deposits, you will have little respect or trust for that person and the relationship will deteriorate. If you deposit more cookies than you withdrawal, it allows for small mistakes, because the jar will still be quite full. The relationship will remain strong."

Dakota said, "I really like that comparison, General. It's easy to take a person for granted. Making deposits is one of the easiest ways to show appreciation and build trust. In the future, I will make a real effort to remember important dates like birthdays and anniversaries. I can mark those dates on my calendar as a reminder. I can send cards or make phone calls when a friend is ill or going through a difficult time."

The General added, "It's also important to keep your promises and take them seriously and deposits work only when they are sincere. People will sense when they are being manipulated"

"I'm going to make a habit of finding a way to make deposits every day," Dakota decided.

The General smiled his approval. "Good!" he said. "I can see you're starting to understand the importance of managing the give-and-take in successful relationships."

He passed the full jar to Dakota. "Let's have some cookies," he laughed.

They leaned back in their chairs and shared a comfortable silence. Munching a cookie, Dakota mulled over the valuable information he had just learned.

After a few minutes, the General broke the silence. "We need to talk about the importance of setting boundaries, Dakota. Boundaries are about what you are willing to tolerate and what you will not accept. Boundaries are a way to protect ourselves from physical and verbal abuse or from being manipulated and used." [1]

He asked Dakota, "Do you think people have boundary issues when they say 'yes' but they mean 'no,' or when they feel others are taking advantage of them, or when they act against their personal values in order to please others?"

"Well, yes," Dakota agreed. He added, "I can relate to a few of those situations myself. I guess when I think I don't have choices; I'm reverting to victim behavior."

"Yes," the General nodded. "That's exactly right. Many foster children and children from dysfunctional families develop non-productive ways to take care of themselves. We all have the right to protect and defend ourselves, and setting boundaries allows us to do that in a positive way.

"Boundaries allow us to establish ground rules that help others know how to treat us and when their behavior is not acceptable," he continued.

"In a relationship, you may want to set a boundary that cheating is not acceptable. You can set a boundary when people borrow things from you. As we learned at the battlefields, children need clear boundaries about their homework, chores, and curfew."

"That's all well and good, General—but what do we do when someone crosses the line?"

"Just as we have the five steps of resolving conflict, we have three steps in setting boundaries," the General replied. He gave Dakota a list to follow along with him as he explained the action plans for setting boundaries.

Setting Boundaries

Action plan number one

Know your motives. Setting a boundary is not about making a threat or an attempt to control the other person. Make sure your request is reasonable.

Be assertive. Give a clear description of the behavior you find unacceptable, without becoming angry or hostile. For example: "You need to take responsibility your budget. I can't lend you any more money."

Be assertive in knowing your limits. For example:
"I'm very busy the next few days. I'm sorry, but I can't help you at this time."
"I'll get back to you on that. I'd like to think about it before giving you an answer."

Action plan number two:

Say what you mean and mean what you say.
Inform the person of a possible consequence if your request continues to be ignored. Do this by giving clear details of the action you will take if the boundaries are not respected.
For example:
"I will not tolerate physical abuse. If you ever hit me again, I will leave or until you get counseling.
"I feel hurt when you break a promise and share personal secrets with others. If this happens again, I will not confide in you again."

Action plan number three:

Be prepared to follow through. Do not state that you will do something, if you're not ready to do it. People will respect your boundaries *only* if you follow through with the consequences. If you carry out steps one and two, but fail at this third step, not only have you wasted your time but also your credibility.

Dakota nodded in agreement. "I understand, General. It's important to let people know when their behavior is not acceptable. When we follow through, we are teaching them how to respect our boundaries. At the same time, we also gain self-respect."

"That's right, Dakota," acknowledged the General. "But boundaries are not about control or manipulation. When we set boundaries, we must be willing to let go of the outcome. Whether the other person wants to accept or agree with the boundary is their choice. People who don't understand boundaries may interpret them as a threat or an ultimatum. Let them know you are sorry they feel that way, but that is not your motive.

"Setting boundaries is more difficult in close or romantic relationships, but they are even more important. The deeper the emotional ties, the harder it may be to set boundaries and follow through with the consequences. We may fear being rejected or losing the relationship and being alone. Remember, Dakota—we always teach others how to treat us."

Dakota thought about this for a moment. Then he said, "It's just like the rules of a game, isn't it? Rules allow for a successful competition, and boundaries allow for a healthy relationship."

The General sat back in his chair. "Well, son," he smiled, "you have almost completed every part of your quest. It's time for you to return to the city and give the gatekeeper your nugget list. Then you are welcome to return here to the ranch for a well-deserved vacation."

"I would like that," replied Dakota. "But wait!—what about drinking from the cup of wisdom?"

"Be patient. That will come," assured the General.

Dakota couldn't hold back the excitement. "I'm ready to go!" he shouted.

"Since you are coming back, you're welcomed to use the jeep.

"By the way," he added. "I called Sunshine before you got up, and I told her you would be in Truth or Consequences this evening. She will be ready to return with you for a few days."

"You old fox!" Dakota grinned.

He jumped up and ran into the cabin to pack a small bag.

"This is the last gatekeeper," Dakota thought, "I don't want to forget anything."

Not knowing what would be expected of him, he packed his manual, treasure chest, and journal. It took only a few minutes get his things together.

The General gave him a warm handshake. "I'll see you and Sunshine tomorrow," he said.

Sunshine was waiting for him at her favorite restaurant. When she got up from her chair, Dakota thought again, "She is so beautiful!" They eagerly shared a long-awaited hug and sat down for dinner.

Dakota couldn't wait to tell her every detail about his adventures in Egypt. "Once I was out of danger and knew my quest was almost compete, I knew I wanted to return to Australia and be part of your life," he eagerly told her. "I couldn't stop thinking about you."

"And I thought about you," Sunshine answered.

He reached for her hand. "I'm glad you did," he smiled.

As the reunion ended, they agreed to meet in the morning for breakfast and leave soon after for the General's ranch.

At Sunshine's front door, Dakota gave her a light kiss. He was floating on air when she returned the kiss.

Back in his hotel room, Dakota resisted the urge to sleep. He wanted to finish his nugget checklist for the gatekeeper and review the notes from his journal.

Dakota removed the conflict resolution list from his treasure chest and added the new learning nuggets for maintaining relationships.

The Learning Nugget Checklist

Maintaining Relationships

- Put *the big rocks in first.*
- Make positive deposits.
- Follow the three-step boundaries action plan.
- Be assertive by giving a clear description of the behavior you find unacceptable, without becoming angry or hostile.
- Identify the consequence if the behavior continues.
- Be prepared to follow through with the consequence.
- Boundaries are not about control or manipulation.
- The deeper the emotional ties, the harder it may be to set boundaries and follow through with the consequence.

Dakota thought about life's treasures. "Life is full of many treasures, but the most precious treasure doesn't lie within any cave or chest. The most priceless treasures lie within each of us, waiting to be discovered.

"How happy I am," Dakota realized as he turned off the lights. "I have a personal treasure chest full of knowledge to change my life and lighten my backpack—and Sunshine cares for me. What more could I want!" With that thought, he fell asleep.

CHAPTER NINE

THE CUP OF WISDOM

Dakota rolled over and turned off the alarm clock. His first thought was, "Today is the day to turn in my last learning nugget checklist—but I haven't drunk from the cup of wisdom."

The General's voice rang in his ear: "Be patient."

Setting aside his worry, he showered, packed, checked out of the hotel, and drove to Sunshine's house for a delicious breakfast.

When the kitchen was cleaned, Sunshine gave Dakota a quick hug. "Thanks for the help," she said. "Now we can leave for the ranch. Do you have your checklist for the gatekeeper?"

"I certainly do," Dakota replied.

He opened the jeep door for Sunshine and they drove to the city gate. The gatekeeper met Dakota with a warm smile.

"Good morning, Dakota! I'm eager to see your checklist!"

Dakota handed over his list. The gatekeeper read it carefully. "Please come with me to my office," he said.

"Oh, no!" Dakota thought. "Have I failed to complete my quest?"

The two men sat across from each other at a desk, the only furniture in the gatekeeper's tiny office.

"Okay" said the gatekeeper, "please tell me the main lessons that you learned on your quest."

Dakota thought for a minute before he answered the gatekeeper's question.

"Life is a continuing quest to live my life the very best way I can and help others along the way.

"If I want my life to be different, I have to do things differently. The road will not always be smooth, so even if I do things differently, I may still have to deal with difficult issues.

"I want to be an action-driven person who takes ownership and responsibility for my life. My actions must be based on sound principles, not emotions.

"I have to keep the learning nuggets in front of me. If I don't use them, I'll lose them and fall back into old patterns from the past.

"Life is an expedition, and I need to challenge and embrace it. With each challenge, there will be opportunity for growth.

"Most important, Uni advised me that I would discover other principles on my journey. I'm starting to understand the meaning behind service. People helping people and giving back can give purpose and meaning to life."

"Well, my friend," said the gatekeeper, "I think you are going to have a bright and happy future."

Dakota replied, "Thank you, sir. I know I'm ready to accept new challenges."

"Excellent," said the gatekeeper as he walked Dakota to the jeep and opened the gate. Then he stepped back and waved him through.

"Good luck and God bless," he called as Dakota and Sunshine drove away.

They drove through the countryside with its striking rock formations, cliffs, and ravines. Dakota felt he was seeing it through different eyes.

Sunshine smiled at Dakota. "We've briefly talked about the fact that I was raised in a very dysfunctional family. Not having a supportive family was a painful experience. My parents were always fighting about something, and on top of that, we moved a lot. It was a lonely place to be, so I decided to create my own family with people I could trust and depend on. What I'm trying to tell you is, I've invited my new extended family to meet us at the General's ranch today. I hope you don't mind."

"Meeting your extended family will mean a lot to me," Dakota replied, "but I don't have an extended family for you to meet, except for Jesse Patterson. He was my mentor back home, and he is the reason I'm on this quest."

"Jesse Patterson!" Sunshine exclaimed. "I know him! The General helped him on his quest when he was here in Australia. Did you know he and his wife got married here? The General was his best man."

Dakota was astonished. "No, he never told me. I'm going to call him and let him know my quest is finished and I've decided to take the job offer here in Australia. I've decided to stay because I've fallen in love with you and I want us to start planning a future together."

Sunshine answered, "Yes, I want that too, Dakota."

As they approached the ranch, Sunshine fell silent. "I hope Dakota will like the surprise we've planned," she thought.

Dakota parked the jeep at the General's front porch. They picked up their luggage and entered the cabin.

The living room was filled with familiar people! "Surprise!" they shouted.

Dakota was stunned. Everyone he had met since he started his quest was there—Uni, Tony and Rhonda, the librarian, and all the gatekeepers crowded around to greet him. The desk clerks, bellmen, and the drivers all greeted him warmly. Even the jogger and his dog had come from Awareness Park! Jack, Ben, and all the other pilots were there. Professor Abu couldn't wait to shake his hand. The captain and the four oarsmen waited patiently with Akua and Uba. Dakota embraced them all.

Then the biggest surprise of all!—Jesse and his family came into the room! Dakota couldn't hold back his emotions. His eyes filled with tears as he said, "I guess this means we're all a family now."

Jesse laughed. "You bet we are."

Dakota was speechless as the General led him toward Uni.

Uni asked, "Dakota, do you have your treasure chest with all your learning nuggets?"

Dakota smiled, "Yes, I certainly do!"

"Good!" Uni said. "I hope you will review them often until they become habits."

He handed Dakota the cup of wisdom and repeated the words spoken by Leonardo DaVinci: "A clever man without wisdom is like a beautiful flower without fragrance."

Uni continued in his own words: "Wisdom is finding the essence of what really matters and the ability to use it to make a difference in the world. If you allow yourself to be pulled away from doing the right thing, you will lose the essence of wisdom."

Then Uni asked, "Do you, Dakota Stone, make a commitment to this family to use common sense and good judgment, and to understand the difference between right and wrong? Do you agree to help others to overcome their emotional baggage?"

"Yes, I do." Dakota promised.

Uni handed him the cup filled with the liquid of wisdom, and Dakota drank.

The General stepped forward with Sunshine to embrace Dakota. "Welcome to the family, son."

Every family member applauded. Holding Sunshine's hand, Dakota thanked his new family for guiding him through his quest.

"I'm honored to be part of this family," he said.

With excitement in his voice, Dakota continued, "Now that you are all here, Sunshine and I want to announce our engagement."

Everyone shouted with joy.

"Jesse, will you be my best man?" he asked.

"Nothing would make me happier," Jesse answered.

The General proudly announced, "And I would be honored to give the bride away."

"Everyone is invited to the wedding in the fall," Sunshine laughed happily.

Uni stepped forward with one last lesson for Dakota and Sunshine. "It's a story to carry in your hearts from this day forward. You can say it wraps up the meaning of your quest, Dakota."

Two Wolves

An old Cherokee told his grandson about a battle that goes on inside all people. He said, "My son, the battle is between two wolves inside us all.

"One wolf is evil. It is anger, envy, jealousy, sorrow, regret, greed, arrogance, self-pity, guilt, resentment, inferiority, lies, false pride, superiority, and ego.

"The other wolf is good. It is joy, peace, love, hope, serenity, humility, kindness, benevolence, empathy, generosity, truth, compassion, and faith."

The grandson thought about the two wolves. Then he turned to his grandfather and asked, "Which wolf wins?"

The old man simply replied, "The one you feed."

Author Unknown

EPILOGUE

REAL-LIFE CROSSROADS

Life presents us with endless choices, and they often come to us as crossroads—moments in time when we struggle with what to do. For many of us, these decisions can be turning points in our lives.

When Thomas Edison was a boy, teachers told him that he was too stupid to learn anything. He became one of the greatest inventors of all time. Michael Jordan is considered by many to be the greatest basketball player in the history of the game, and he was cut from his high school team. Walt Disney was fired by a newspaper editor who told him he lacked imagination and had no good ideas, but he created Mickey Mouse and many other well-loved characters.

When we believe in ourselves and have internal motivation, our crossroads can define who we can become. But we won't know where the road leads until we decide to take it.

My motivation for change was realizing that what's in my backpack not only affects me, but those around me. The changes I make in my life can influence others in a positive way. Consequently, I can make a difference in helping others make positive changes in their lives.

The following stories are examples of people who listened to their inner voice and had the motivation to move in a new direction.

Hugo's Crossroad

Hugo, a mentor for foster youth, became a father while still in the system. When he turned eighteen and transitioned out of foster care, he had no support system. It was a stressful and confusing time for him.

Without help, he turned to gangs and drugs. This was the only way he knew to survive.

Now an adult, Hugo has put all that behind him. I asked him what led him to that decision. He told me that while holding his child one day, he decided that he didn't want to be like his own father. He visualized being a good father. With that visualization, words of affirmation, and a deep desire to change, Hugo is achieving his goal of becoming a supportive parent. Sometimes he makes mistakes, but he has learned from those mistakes and continues to move forward.

Both Hugo and I have experienced foster care, and our experiences have created a bond between us. Never underestimate the value of sharing your story with someone else who has "been there." Together, we can grow and help others to overcome painful experiences.

Natalie's Crossroad

Natalie became a survivor of abusive foster care and "special ed" classes. As a result, she was illiterate at the age of eighteen. One after-school activity that she could participate in without having to read was a class in sign language. That class would change her life.

As a young adult, she lived at the YWCA, where many of the other residents were deaf. Word quickly spread among those residents that there was a woman living there who could sign *and* talk. She became a communication link and a great friend to many. Realizing the need for a translator and the service it provided, she became determined to learn how to read and write. She found a tutor through the local university. At the age of 21, she entered that university as a student. Graduation with honors was followed by a scholarship and a move to Los Angeles to earn her Master's degree in social work.

Natalie dedicated the next two decades of her life to the cause of the disabled. While her focus was the deaf, she was instrumental in developing the legislation that became the Americans with Disabilities Act.

Natalie reached her crossroad when she found a cause outside of herself. The desire to serve others accomplished what her middle school, high school, and foster care experiences could not. She is currently writing a book titled, *My Journey in Signs.*

Lu's Crossroad

During Lu's high school years, she lived in six different foster homes or institutions and attended five different schools. She was repeatedly told she would not graduate. The constant verbal abuse wore down her self-esteem.

Lu was at a crossroad. Should she continue to believe the predictions that she would never finish high school? Would she prove that they were wrong? At some point, she decided to prove everyone wrong. "I just got tired of hearing it," she said. She gave herself the motivation and determination to succeed against tremendous odds. Not only did she graduate from high school, but after she aged out of foster care she met the challenges and graduated from college. With no support system, she found a way. She successfully took the negative predictions of others and used them as the motivation to succeed.

Lu's advice to other foster youth is, "If you can believe in yourself, you can find the motivation and determination to overcome obstacles, one day at a time."

Lu's and Her Sister Valeria's Crossroad

Siblings can give each other a feeling of belonging and can supply each other with emotional permanence. Lu believes one of the worst things that can happen to children is to lose contact with their siblings. Lu and her sister Valeria knew the pain of being separated. The damage to their relationship was evident when both aged out of the system. The process of regaining the closeness of two sisters would take years.

Lu and Valeria were standing at a crossroad. Would they manage the emotional stress required to rebuild their relationship? Or would they decide to live with the pain of never trying? They decided to rebuild what was taken away from them.

Lu and Valeria overcame many of the roadblocks created by being separated. Now they are able to build memories, share secrets, and celebrate wonderful family events.

This book doesn't have all the answers, which is why there are trained specialists to help mend the brokenness. But the learning nuggets helped me to rebuild a better life after a shattered childhood. I hope they will help you, to turn your rocks into gems and your scars into stars.

POEMS TO INSPIRE

One

One song can spark a moment
One flower can wake the dream
One tree can start a forest
One bird can herald spring
One smile begins a friendship
One handclasp lifts a soul
One star can guide a ship at sea
One word can frame the goal
One vote can change a nation
One sunbeam lights a room
One candle wipes out darkness
One laugh will conquer gloom
One step must start each journey
One word must start a prayer
One hope will raise our spirits
One touch can show you care
One voice can speak with wisdom
One heart can know what's true
One life can make a difference.

Unknown

HAPPINESS

Happiness,
Isn't the amount of clothes hanging in my closet,
For if that is true, I'm afraid, I've already lost it.
I can't drink it, swallow it or snort it.
For these things will only distort it.

Happiness can't be found in a relationship
Based only on sex or good looks.
You can't find it in a storybook.

I may be blessed with a talent given to me at birth,
But talent alone can't create happiness and worth.

Happiness isn't about the color of my skin
It's my attitude within that makes me grin.

JB Woak

The Garden of Life

Picture in your mind a garden.
Let's say this garden represents your life.

God has provided you with a special handbook,
To insure the quality of your garden.

The gardener that sows the seeds of
Positive principles will reap the harvest of:

Faith to supersede doubt
Joy to replace sorrow
Peacefulness to end anxiety & stress
Hopefulness to uproot discouragement
Forgiveness to eliminate hostility & bitterness
Harmony to resolve conflict
Endurance to prevent wavering
Patience to over ride quick cures
Stewardship in serving others
Love that shows compassion & mercy

Be careful,
For your outer expression will often mirror
What has been rooted within the heart.

To improve the quality of your garden
Re-evaluate the principles sown within.

JB Woak

Attitude Shift

There are many storms in life we cannot escape,
But how I choose to react,
Is something I have the power to shape.

A downcast face, my friend, doesn't just happen.
Its sour thoughts,
That will keep you from laugh'en.

To continue to dwell upon past hurts and pains,
Will only insure,
That your feelings will remain the same.

You can rise above hurts and disappointments,
When your heart is full of sorrow.
By choosing love and forgiveness,
Will bring you a brighter tomorrow.

If your life needs a face-lift,
Try an attitude shift.

Heavenly Father,
Warm our hearts with your strength and
Give us the courage to face the storms of life.
Help us to focus on what we can do and the how to.

JB Woak

Our House

Within our house are loved ones
Whose feelings are within our care.
Yet often,
The temperament of our attitude can
Be felt without a word to share.

Feelings can be turned into expressions of love.
When our attitudes come from
Our Heavenly Father above.

May we cherish our house and the
People within our reach.
To be careful with our expressions
And the tone of our speech.

Lord help us to temper our attitude
With respect and kindness each day.
Teach us to love with our hearts,
When our feelings get in the way.

JB Woak

Fences

Throughout my life, I have built many fences,
And they come in many different forms.
My fences have become a barrier
To hide my fears.

Some fences are extremely high.
They hide the brokenness & pains of the past.
Broken and violated children,
Left with a soul that has been robbed of
Self worth and a lost sense of identity.

Now in the present,
My faith will shape my future.
My choices will define
Who and what I am or will become.

Dear Heavenly Father
Help us to build healthy boundaries
That maintains personal integrity and self-respect.

Help us to embrace the brokenness and pains of the past.
Help us to find love and acceptance of who we are.
Help us to transform those difficult barriers so
We can find true freedom and love.

Heavenly Father,
Give us the courage to take back
The ownership of life.
Through Your word.

JB Woak

BOOKS THAT INSPIRE CHANGE

The first thing I had to learn was the concept of being teachable—learning new ways to do things. Here are some books that inspired me to be a better person.

Allen, James. 2006. *As a Man Thinketh.* New York: Penguin Group
Burney, Robert. 1998. *Codependence: The Dance of Wounded Souls.* Encinitas: Joy to You & Me Enterprises.
Carpenter, Harry W. 2004. *The Genie Within: Your Subconscious Mind.* San Diego: Anaphase II Publishing.
Cloud, Henry, and Townsend, John. 2002. *Boundaries.* Grand Rapids: Zonbervan.
Covey, Stephen R. 1997. *The 7 Habits of Highly Effective Families.* New York: Golden Books.
Frankl, Viktor E. 2006. *Man's Search for Meaning .Boston:* Beacon Press.
George, Bill. 2007. *True North.* San Francisco: Wiley Imprint.
Hill, Napoleon.1995 *Grow Rich! With Peace of Mind.* New York: Ballantine Books.
Josephson, Michael. 2002. *Making Ethical Decision.* Los Angeles: Josephson Institute of Ethics.
Lerner, Harriet. 2005. *The Dance of Anger.* New York: Harper-Collins Publisher.
Lewis, Barbara. 2005. *What Do You Stand For? Teen Building Character.* Minneapolis: Free Spirit Publishing.
Maxwell, C. John, and Dornan, Jim Maxwell. 1997. *Becoming A Person of Influence.* Nashville: Thomas Nelson.
Maltz, Dr. Maxwell. 1969. *Psycho-Cybernetics.* New York: Pocket Books.
McGraw, Dr. Phil. 2004. *Family First.* New York: Free Press.

Minirth, Frank, and Meier, Paul. 1994. *Happiness Is a Choice. Grand Rapids: Baker Publishing Group.*

Nightingale, Earl. 1993. *The Essence of Success. Chicago:Nightingale-Conant.*

Schuller, Robert H. 1983. *Tough Times Never Last, But Tough People Do! Nashville: Thomas Nelson.*

Swindoll, Charles R. 1998. *Strengthening Your Grip. Nashville: W Publishing Group.*

Waitley, Denis. 1995. *The Psychology of Winning. New York: Simon and Schuster.*

Warren, Rick. 2002. *The Purpose Driven Life. Grand Rapids: Zonbervan.*

Ziglar, Zig. 2006. *Better Than Good: Creating a Life You Can't Wait to Live. Nashville: Thomas Nelson Inc.*

Life Application Bible. Grand Rapids: Zondervan

REFERENCES

Chapter Two

[1] Shaprio, Phil. *The Story of the Six Blind Men. Modernized and retold.* http://www.philipshapiro.com/. Accessed 2009.

Chapter Three

[1] Maltz, Maxwell, M.D., F.I.C.S. 1973. *Psycho-Cybernetics.* New York: Pocket Books, a division of Simon & Schuster: 28

Chapter Five

[1] Swindoll, Charles R. 1982. *Strengthening Your Grip.* Nashville: W Publishing Group: 195

Chapter Eight

[1] Burney, Robert. 1998. *Codependence: The Dance of Wounded Souls.* Encinitas: Joy to You & Me Enterprises.